A PASSION FOR VEGETABLES

A PASSION FOR VEGETABLES

LORENZA DE'MEDICI

PHOTOGRAPHS BY MIKE NEWTON

PAVILION

First published in Great Britain in 2002 by
PAVILION BOOKS LIMITED
64 Brewery Road
London N7 9NT
www.chrysalisbooks.co.uk

A member of **Chrysalis** Books plc

Home Economist Bridget Sargeson
Designed by David Fordham

A CIP catalogue record for this book is available
from the British Library

ISBN 1 86205 478 9

Set in Bell and Serlio by MATS, Southend-on-Sea, Essex
Printed in Singapore by Kyodo Printing Co. PTE Ltd.

2 4 6 8 10 9 7 5 3 1

This book can be ordered direct from the publisher. Please contact
the Marketing Department. But try your bookshop first.

CONTENTS

INTRODUCTION

I HAVE OFTEN BEEN "ACCUSED" of being a vegetarian, in times past by my more carnivorous children who thought I unfairly weighed the family meals in favour of vegetables and, more recently, by participants in my cooking classes, who wonder why I don't do more meat dishes. The truth of the matter is they are right. I have a preference for greens and fresh vegetables, not because of any philosophical bias or even health concerns. It is simply a passion and passions, as we all know, are not subject to reason. Not too long ago when some of my friends and neighbours in Tuscany were in a panic about the European ban on certain cuts of meat, I have to say my personal eating habits were not in the least affected. Thanks to my vegetable garden at Badia a Coltibuono, our family wine estate in Tuscany, and my local market, I could get along just fine on a purely vegetarian diet.

Before you prepare the recipes in this book here are a couple of preliminaries. First of all, invest in a bottle of the finest extra-virgin olive oil you can find. Better still make that two bottles. The first will go quickly. I recommend extra-virgin olive oil from the Chianti Classico region of Tuscany, estate produced and bottled It has a deliciously full and fruity flavour. I use the extra-virgin olive oil produced on our estate. The essential factor is that the olive oil be of the highest quality. Inferior olive oil will ruin your best efforts. Superior extra-virgin olive oil guarantees success.

Only use seasonal produce. This takes some unlearning of old habits and some discipline but only at first. When you get used to the satisfying taste of fresh vegetables at the height of their season, you will not even consider using watery tomatoes in winter. Much better to take out your preserves and wait until summer to put tomatoes on the table. Before thinking about your menu, go to the garden or the local market, hopefully a farmer's market, and see which vegetables look the most promising. I have learned to head straight for the stalls that sell local and organic produce. It might not look as glamorous as some of the perfectly shaped and glossy coloured treated produce but for flavour it cannot be beaten.

Only after you have brought your greens and vegetables home, is it time to consult the recipes in this book. I hope you find many recipes and ideas for vegetable dishes that will give you satisfaction in the kitchen and much pleasure to your family and friends at the table.

LEAVES, STALKS
& SPROUTS

ASPARAGUS

(OFFICINALIS)

"*Quicker than asparagus is boiled*"

(A ROMAN PROVERB MEANING "IN A FLASH")

ASPARAGUS STALKS, also called spears, are the first shoots to spring up in my garden, usually by early April. All of a sudden there they are, fully grown, looking a little thin and naked in the still chilly air. Harbingers of spring, they arrive even earlier in local markets. You will see three types – white, purple and green. Asparagus are kept white by a process called blanching. Gardeners bank earth around them so their shoots remain underground, hidden from the sun. The ones with purple spears are picked as soon as they emerge from the soil. Green asparagus is the most common and the tastiest, because its flavour, as well as its colour, has had time to fully develop.

The best white Italian asparagus comes from the north-eastern regions of the country, the Veneto and Friuli. The town of Bassano, not far from Venice, is celebrated for its native white asparagus, *bianco di Bassano*. Their tender stalks are as thick as a thumb and edible from plump top to plump bottom. A delicious regional dish is risotto, another culinary speciality of the area, made with white asparagus. The stalks are chopped and cooked with the rice and the tips are added at the end along with Parmesan cheese and butter.

Green asparagus is prepared in many tasty ways. When I was growing up in Milan, the family took an annual spring drive on a sunny Sunday to the town of Cantello, near the Swiss border, which, I remember, had a sign at its entrance announcing, *La Capitale Degli Asparagi*, The Capital of Asparagus. For lunch we would have asparagus cooked in a way I have since often prepared at home for my family – boiled then topped with butter and Parmesan and briefly baked.

Tuscans, traditionally and still avid foragers, gather wild asparagus, called *asparagi di campo*. These are pencil thin and intensely flavoured, full of vitamins and minerals, and grow along sandy roadsides. Sometimes you will find them at country markets. A favourite way to use them is in a *frittata*, an Italian omelette.

With regard to preparing asparagus for cooking (usually by boiling or steaming), in this as in most other cases, I belong to the school that favours the quick and easy method of simply cutting off the tough and often sandy ends. Since it is perfectly permissible, in fact recommendable, to pick up asparagus spears with your fingers, the harder base that is left provides a convenient handle for eating the tender tips.

ASPARAGUS WITH OIL AND LEMON
Asparagi all'agro

1KG/2¼LB ASPARAGUS
JUICE OF 1 LEMON
6 TBSP EXTRA-VIRGIN OLIVE OIL
SALT AND PEPPER

Bring a large saucepan of water to the boil. Peel the asparagus stems with a potato peeler and tie them in a bundle with kitchen string. Stand the bundle in the water to just barely cover the green tops and cook for about 10 minutes, or until the tops begin to bend. Remove from the pan, untie them, and arrange on a platter. Sprinkle with salt and pepper, pour over the lemon juice and the oil and serve, immediately or at room temperature.

Serves 6

ASPARAGUS WITH EGGS AND PARMESAN CHEESE
Asparagi alla parmigiana

1KG/2¼LB ASPARAGUS
90G/3OZ/6 TBSP UNSALTED BUTTER
6 LARGE EGGS
6 TBSP FRESHLY GRATED
PARMESAN CHEESE
SALT AND PEPPER

Bring a large saucepan of water to the boil. Peel the asparagus stems with a potato peeler and tie them in a bundle with kitchen string. Stand the bundle in the water to just barely cover the green tops and cook for about 10 minutes, or until the tops begin to bend. Remove from the pan, untie them, arrange on a platter and keep them warm. Melt the butter in a non-stick pan and fry the eggs sunny-side up. Arrange them on top of the asparagus. Sprinkle with salt and pepper and the Parmesan cheese and pour on top the butter in which the eggs were fried. Serve immediately.

Serves 6

ASPARAGUS TART
TORTA DI ASPARAGI

300G/10OZ/2 CUPS PLAIN (ALL-PURPOSE)
FLOUR, PLUS EXTRA FOR DUSTING
150G/5OZ/10 TBSP UNSALTED BUTTER
1KG/2¼LB ASPARAGUS
3 LARGE EGGS
120ML/4FL OZ/½ CUP DOUBLE
(HEAVY) CREAM
6 TBSP FRESHLY GRATED
PARMESAN CHEESE
SALT AND PEPPER

Grease and flour the base and sides of a loose-bottomed 23cm/9in tart tin, shaking off any excess flour.

Using your fingertips, work the flour into the butter until well combined then form into a ball. Roll out the dough and use to line the tin then place in the refrigerator for about 2 hours.

Preheat the oven to 170°C/350°F/ gas mark 3.

Discard the stems of the asparagus and blanch the tips in boiling, salted water for about 3 minutes. Drain the asparagus tips and arrange in concentric circles on top of the dough. Beat the eggs with the cream and a little salt and pepper and pour on top of the asparagus. Sprinkle with the Parmesan cheese. Cook the tart in the oven until golden, about 40 minutes. Leave in the tin to cool slightly then demould on to a platter and serve warm or at room temperature.

Serves 6

CAULIFLOWER

(BRASSICA OLERACEA BOTRYTI)

"Cauliflower is nothing but cabbage with a college education."

(MARK TWAIN 1835–1910)

IN SOUTHERN ITALY broccoli is often called *cavolfiori*, while in other regions of the country *cavolfiori* means cauliflower. This may be confusing when ordering in a restaurant but when preparing most recipes you can use these two vegetables interchangeably. They are both members of the same species, relatives of the cabbage family. Cauliflowers are the most colourful cousins of the group, which includes, besides cabbage and broccoli, Brussels sprouts and kale.

Cultivated cauliflower consists of a tight cluster of the edible flower stems of the mother plant, *Brassica oleracea*, which have not yet flowered, much the same as broccoli. These develop into the common large white head and smaller varieties that are purple, pale green and white. In good produce markets they come surrounded by beautiful long and tender bluish-green leaves, which add flavour when the cauliflower is cooked. The head should be compact and firm and the flower buds compressed. Both cauliflower and broccoli are exceptionally rich in vitamins and minerals, because they still contain all the nutrients that would have gone into their flowers and fruits.

Cauliflower is another vegetable whose appeal is greatly enhanced by a dressing of fine extra-virgin olive oil and good quality wine vinegar. For a quick, healthy and satisfying light lunch, I divide the head into florets, steam them *al dente* and toss with the olive oil dressing. I find this preparation far superior than serving cauliflower with a white or hollandaise sauce. If I want to dress up this dish for company, after cooking the cauliflower, I sprinkle the florets with red grapes and walnuts and season with paprika. *Cavolfiore gratinato*, cauliflower au gratin, browned with butter and Parmesan, is a dish worthy of the finest dinner. When I find a very tender cauliflower, mild and fresh – early winter is their best season, I like to use it raw, in a salad or as one of the dipping vegetables for *bagna cauda* (see p.42 cardoons). In both dishes a few anchovy fillets combine well with the flavour of cauliflower.

CAULIFLOWER WITH GRAPES
Cavolfiore con uva

1 CAULIFLOWER OF ABOUT 1KG/2¼LB,
TRIMMED
210G/7OZ SEEDLESS BLACK GRAPES,
WASHED
4 TBSP EXTRA-VIRGIN OLIVE OIL
1 TSP SWEET PAPRIKA
60G/2OZ CHOPPED WALNUTS
SALT

Bring a large saucepan of salted water to the boil. Lower the cauliflower into the pan, keeping the top of the florets barely covered. Cook for about 10 minutes, drain and let cool. Divide into florets and arrange on a serving dish. Scatter the grapes over the cauliflower. Pour the oil over the cauliflower and grapes and sprinkle with the paprika and chopped walnuts. Serve at room temperature.

Serves 6

CAULIFLOWER WITH HAZELNUTS
Cavolfiore alle nocciole

1 CAULIFLOWER OF ABOUT 1KG/2¼LB,
TRIMMED
90G/3OZ SWEET BUTTER
90G/3OZ HAZELNUTS, PEELED
AND CHOPPED
SALT

Bring a large saucepan of lightly salted water to the boil. Lower the cauliflower into the pan, keeping the top of the florets barely covered. Cook for about 10 minutes, drain and divide into three florets. Arrange on a serving dish and keep warm. Cook the butter and the hazelnuts until golden, about three minutes. Pour over the cauliflower and serve immediately.

Serves 6

CAULIFLOWER WITH OLIVES
Cavolfiore alle olive

1 CAULIFLOWER OF ABOUT 1KG/2¼LB,
TRIMMED
180G/6OZ GAETA OR KALAMATA
OLIVES, STONED
3 ANCHOVY FILLETS IN OIL
6 TBSP EXTRA-VIRGIN OLIVE OIL
1 TBSP FRESH BREADCRUMBS
2 TBSP RED WINE VINEGAR
1 HARD-BOILED (HARD-COOKED) EGG,
FINELY CHOPPED
3 TBSP FINELY CHOPPED FLAT-LEAF
ITALIAN PARSLEY
SALT

Bring a large saucepan of lightly salted water to the boil. Lower the cauliflower into the pan, keeping the top of the florets barely covered. Cook for about 10 minutes, drain and divide into florets. Place in a serving dish, add the olives and keep warm. Mash the anchovies with the oil. Soak the breadcrumbs in the vinegar and squeeze dry. Add to the anchovies and oil with the hard-boiled (hard-cooked) egg and the parsley. Mix well, pour on top of the cauliflower and serve at room temperature or lukewarm.

Serves 6

CAULIFLOWER AU GRATIN
Cavolfiore gratinato

1 CAULIFLOWER OF ABOUT 1KG/2¼LB,
TRIMMED
25G/1OZ/2 TBSP UNSALTED BUTTER
4 TBSP PLAIN (ALL-PURPOSE) FLOUR
600ML/1 PINT/2 CUPS MILK
6 TBSP FRESHLY GRATED PARMESAN
CHEESE
1 LARGE PINCH OF GRATED NUTMEG
SALT AND PEPPER

Preheat the oven to 200°C/400°F/gas mark 6.

Bring a large saucepan of salted water to the boil. Lower the cauliflower into the water to barely cover and cook for about 10 minutes. Drain and keep whole. Arrange on a heatproof soufflé dish. Melt the butter in a saucepan, add the flour and cook over a medium heat, stirring with a wooden spoon, for about 3 minutes. Add the milk a little at a time, stirring continuously, until a creamy, velvety sauce is formed. Take off the heat and add the cheese and salt and pepper to taste. Mix until well incorporated. Pour the sauce over the cauliflower and sprinkle with the nutmeg. Cook in the oven for about 15 minutes, or until bubbling and slightly golden on top. Serve very hot.

Serves 6

BROCCOLI

(BRASSICA OLERACEA ITALICA}

IT IS SAID THAT SOME PEOPLE do not like broccoli. My solution to that problem would be to serve them broccoli as a dressing for short pasta – penne or fusilli, for example. All you need do is boil the broccoli *al dente* (save the flavoured water for cooking the pasta), roughly chop the florets and stalks and sauté them in olive oil and garlic. Add freshly ground black pepper or a sprinkle of chilli pepper flakes and conversion is guaranteed.

Along with cauliflower, to which it is closely related, broccoli is the most attractive and colourful member of the otherwise rather drab, domestic cabbage family. Actually broccoli is a cabbage that has gone wild, as it were, and formed flowers that have started to bud. As its name suggests, broccoli is another vegetable that was developed in Italy. Besides the most common variety with dark green heads and small stalks, several other kinds with distinctive colours and shapes liven up Italian winter market stalls and cold weather dishes. The most exotic, called *Romanesco*, produces conical chartreuse heads with spiralling florets and has a more delicate flavour than the common kind.

When you buy broccoli, look for heads with compact florets and vivid colour with no yellowing buds, and make sure the stalks are firm. In farmers' markets you will find heads with the leaves still attached – these leaves, and the stalks, can be cooked with the broccoli florets for added flavour. Since broccoli is famously rich in nutrients and in antidotes to various maladies, it is best cooked briefly in just a little water or steamed, *al dente*. It will also look and taste much better than if it is overboiled or waterlogged. It can then be sautéed or stir-fried according to the recipe. I find that broccoli has an affinity for anchovies, a taste of which I often add to a simple dressing of extra-virgin olive oil.

An offshoot of broccoli, *broccoletti* in Italian meaning, literally, "little broccoli" and always popular here, is now becoming popular in other parts of the world. *Broccoletti* are greens of the broccoli family with tiny, thin stalks that have started to flower. They have a distinctive flavour all of their own, nutty or peppery and slightly bitter, and are prepared in the same way as broccoli. This same name is also given to greens very similar to turnip tops, *cime di rape*.

BROCCOLI AND BEAN SOUP
PASSATO DI BROCCOLI E FAGIOLI

210G/7OZ DRIED CANNELLINI
(WHITE) BEANS
750G/1½LB BROCCOLI
6 TBSP EXTRA-VIRGIN OLIVE OIL
120G/4OZ BACON, CHOPPED
6 GARLIC CLOVES, CHOPPED
SALT AND PEPPER

Put the beans in a bowl, cover with water and soak for 12 hours. Drain. Peel the broccoli stems and slice them. Put the beans into a saucepan with about 2 litres/3½ pints/8 cups of water and slowly bring to the boil. Cook them for 1½ hours, then add the broccoli stems and florets and cook for about 10 minutes. Reserve a few broccoli florets for decoration and pass everything else through a foodmill. (Do not blend in a processor as the texture will be too smooth.) To serve, reheat the purée and add salt to taste. Heat the oil in a pan and fry the bacon and garlic until barely golden. Pour the broccoli purée into a soup tureen, add the oil, bacon and garlic and mix well. Sprinkle with pepper, decorate with the reserved broccoli florets and serve.

Serves 6

BROCCOLI WITH ANCHOVY SAUCE
BROCCOLI ALL'ACCIUGATA

1KG/2¼LB BROCCOLI
6 ANCHOVY FILLETS IN SALT
3 TBSP EXTRA-VIRGIN OLIVE OIL
3 GARLIC CLOVES, CHOPPED

Discard the stems of the broccoli (they can be used for a soup) and divide the florets. Clean and well rinse the anchovies and chop roughly. Heat the oil in a pan, add the garlic and anchovies and fry over a low heat until the anchovies have dissolved and the garlic is barely golden. Add 2 tablespoons of water, to stop the cooking, mix well and set aside. Bring a large saucepan of water to the boil, add the broccoli florets and cook for about 3 minutes. Drain them, reserving a little of the cooking water, and add them to the pan with the anchovies. Reheat, shaking the pan, and add a few tablespoons of the cooking water. Heat through for about 5 minutes, then arrange the broccoli on a platter and serve.

Serves 6

BROCCOLI WITH BREADCRUMBS
BROCCOLI AL PANGRATTATO

1KG/2¼LB BROCCOLI
6 TBSP EXTRA-VIRGIN OLIVE OIL
6 TBSP SOFT BREADCRUMBS
3 GARLIC CLOVES, CHOPPED
6 TBSP GRATED SMOKED
PROVOLONE CHEESE
SALT AND PEPPER

Discard the stems of the broccoli (they can be used for a soup) and divide the florets. Bring a large saucepan of salted water to the boil, immerse the broccoli and cook for about 3 minutes. Drain and keep the broccoli warm. Heat 3 tablespoons of the oil in a non-stick pan, add the breadcrumbs and garlic and fry, stirring continuously, until barely golden. Arrange the broccoli on a platter, sprinkle over the remaining oil, the pepper, grated cheese and finally the breadcrumbs and serve immediately.

Serves 6

BRUSSELS SPROUTS

(BRASSICA OLERACEA GEMMIFERA)

Brussels sprouts are another member of the many-branched cabbage family. In Italy we call them *cavolini di Bruxelles*, little cabbages from Brussels. According to tradition they originated in Italy and were brought to Brussels, not, in this case, by Caterina de'Medici, but many centuries before by the occupying Roman legions. From old recipe books it would seem they were forgotten, or at least widely neglected, in the gardens and kitchens of our peninsula until the nineteenth century. Now they are once again quite popular.

Brussels sprouts grow along a thick stalk about 1 metre/ 3 feet in height topped with several large leaves. Its numerous little green or red buds, resembling perfectly formed miniature cabbages, are harvested when they reach the size of a walnut. For a decorative addition to your kitchen, go to a farmers' market and see if you can find the entire exotic-looking stalk. Keep it in a cool corner with its feet in water and you can pick off the sprouts whenever you need them.

Like their cousin broccoli, Brussels sprouts taste best when lightly cooked in little water. They have a delicate and sweet flavour that is easily waterlogged by too much boiling. The simplest way to prepare them is to sauté them for a few minutes in olive oil and a little broth, then season with salt and pepper. Unless they are very tiny, I cut them in half before cooking. The most traditional recipe for Brussels sprouts, said to have originated in Brussels itself, combines boiled chestnuts with buttered sprouts. This is a classic side dish served with Christmas turkey and goes well with all roast fowl and meats.

A few years ago I was served a delicious dish of dried pasta at the Chez Panisse Café, Alice Waters' celebrated restaurant in Berkeley, California. It was simply dressed with olive oil and little greens, which I was not able to identify, neither by their shape, nor by their taste. She told me they were Brussels sprouts. The cook (energetic, young prep-cooks, I'm sure) had separated the individual leaves of the sprout and then they were sautéed. For some reason this method gives them an additional nutty flavour. I have never tried it myself but if you have the time and patience, or a willing sous-chef at hand, it is a dish that will be a pleasant surprise to your family and friends.

BRUSSELS SPROUTS COOKED IN BEER

Cavolini di Bruxelles alla birra

750G/1½LB BRUSSELS SPROUTS,
TRIMMED
120ML/4FL OZ/½ CUP BEER
3 TBSP EXTRA-VIRGIN OLIVE OIL
3 HARD-BOILED (HARD-COOKED) EGGS
2 TBSP CHOPPED FLAT-LEAF
ITALIAN PARSLEY
SALT AND PEPPER

Blanch the sprouts for 1 minute in a saucepan of boiling water. Drain them then place in a large saucepan with the beer and the oil. Cook uncovered over a medium heat for about 10 minutes, or until tender and the beer has been absorbed. Meanwhile, pass the egg yolks through a sieve, and finely chop the egg whites. Add salt and pepper to the sprouts to taste, then arrange them on a platter. Sprinkle on the parsley and the egg yolks, surround with the chopped egg whites, and serve.

Serves 6

BRUSSELS SPROUTS WITH CURRY

Cavolini di Bruxelles al curry

360G/12OZ BRUSSELS SPROUTS, TRIMMED
360G/12OZ BABY (PEARL) ONIONS, TRIMMED
1 HANDFUL DARK RAISINS
1 COOKING APPLE, PEELED, CORED AND DICED
120ML/4FL OZ/½ CUP DOUBLE (HEAVY) CREAM
2 TBSP CURRY POWDER
SALT

Blanch the sprouts for 1 minute in a saucepan of boiling water. Drain, then return to the pan with the onions. Add the raisins and the apple. Pour in the cream and sprinkle with salt to taste and the curry powder. Cover and cook over a low heat for about 15 minutes, stirring gently from time to time, until the sprouts are tender and the cream has been absorbed. Arrange on a platter and serve.

Serves 6

BRUSSELS SPROUTS WITH CHESTNUTS

Cavolini di Bruxelles alle castagne

360G/12OZ BRUSSELS SPROUTS,
TRIMMED
480G/1LB CHESTNUTS
90G/3OZ/6 TBSP UNSALTED BUTTER
LARGE PINCH OF GRATED NUTMEG
SALT

Cook the sprouts in a saucepan of boiling, salted water for about 10 minutes, until tender. Drain and keep them warm. Make an incision in the chestnuts and boil them in salted water for about 20 minutes, until tender. Drain, peel and keep them warm. Melt the butter in a saucepan but do not let it brown. Arrange the chestnuts and sprouts on a platter, pour the melted butter on top, sprinkle with the grated nutmeg and serve.

Serves 6

CABBAGES

(BRASSICA OLERACEA CAPITATA)

*"Few and signally blest are those whom Jupiter has destined
to be cabbage-planters.
For they've always one foot on the ground, and the other not far from it."*

(FRANCOIS RABELAIS C.1542–1553, PANURGE IV. 18)

ALPHABETICALLY it comes after broccoli and Brussels sprouts but botanically it comes before. Cabbage, in fact, was the first vegetable of the genus *Brassica* to be cultivated from the wild and is the ancestor not only of broccoli and Brussels sprouts but of cauliflower, kohlrabi, kale, mustard greens and several other species as well. The Greeks and Romans esteemed its health-giving properties and it had already been around a long time before them. It would seem from archaeological evidence that the ancient Celts, living along the coasts of Brittany and Normandy, were the first to introduce wild cabbage into their daily diet. The first cultivated cabbage was loose-leaf. Today's headed cabbage was developed in northern Europe around the First Century BC.

As its lineage testifies, cabbage is a venerable vegetable, though its reputation has suffered over the course of the centuries. This is due in part to the fact that it has become so commonplace, but mostly, I would guess, because of unimaginative preparation. It comes as a surprise to those who associate cabbage exclusively with the restricted winter diet of peoples living in cold climes, to discover that it is popular in Italian cooking, where there are so many other greens available. *Cavolo nero*, dark cabbage, is an essential ingredient in authentic Tuscan soups and cabbage is stewed with meat dishes, pork in particular. I stuff its leaves with meat and braise them.

Extra-virgin olive oil can do a lot to enhance the appeal of plain cabbage. Shaved raw cabbage, dressed with olive oil and lemon juice, is a good topping or base for *carpaccio*-type dishes – sliced raw fillet of beef covered with flakes of Parmesan. For the Prince and the Pauper effect, add sliced truffles.

Many Italian recipes using cabbage are from the northern borders with Switzerland, Austria and Yugoslavia. They often combine cabbage with pork products, especially lardons and spare ribs. In Lombardia pork with cabbage is accompanied by polenta.

RED CABBAGE WITH APPLES
CAVOLO ROSSO ALLE MELE

3 TBSP EXTRA-VIRGIN OLIVE OIL
1 RED CABBAGE OF ABOUT 1KG/2¼LB, THINLY SLICED
60ML/2FL OZ/4 TBSP RED WINE VINEGAR
2 APPLES, GOLDEN DELICIOUS OR SIMILAR, PEELED AND SLICED
SALT AND PEPPER

Heat the oil in a saucepan, add the cabbage, mix well and cook, covered, over a low heat for about 10 minutes. Add salt and pepper to taste, pour in the vinegar, cover again and cook for 1 hour more. Add the apples to the cabbage and cook for 10 minutes more. If necessary, add a little water to keep the cooking juices barely moist. Arrange on a platter and serve.

Serves 6

WHITE CABBAGE SAUTEED WITH GARLIC
CAVOLELLA ALL'AGLIO

6 TBSP EXTRA-VIRGIN OLIVE OIL
6 GARLIC CLOVES, CHOPPED
600G/1¼LB WHITE CABBAGE, THINLY SLICED
SALT AND PEPPER

Heat the oil in a large saucepan, add the garlic and cook over a medium heat for about 3 minutes until translucent. Add the cabbage and sauté over a high heat, stirring constantly, for 3 minutes more, until wilted. Add salt and pepper to taste and serve immediately.

Serves 6

SAVOY CABBAGE WITH SPARE RIBS
CAVOLO VERZA CON COSTOLECCIO

2 TBSP EXTRA-VIRGIN OLIVE OIL
120G/4OZ PANCETTA, DICED
2 WHITE ONIONS, SLICED
600G/1¼LB PORK SPARE RIBS
120G/4OZ SAUSAGES
600G/1¼LB SAVOY CABBAGE,
THINLY SLICED
1 LITRE/1¾ PINT/4 CUPS
VEGETABLE STOCK
SALT AND PEPPER

Heat the oil in a large saucepan and sauté the pancetta and onions for about 3 minutes over a medium heat until translucent. Add the pork ribs and the sausages and sauté, stirring occasionally, for 5 minutes more. Add the cabbage, stock and salt and pepper to taste, then cover and cook over a low heat for about 2 hours. The liquid will reduce by half. Arrange in a bowl and serve.

Serves 6

CHARD & SPINACH

(BETA VULGARIS CICLA & SPINACIA OLERACEA)

"One man's poison ivy is another man's spinach"

(GEORGE ADE, "THE BRAND THAT WAS PLUCKED", *HAND-MADE FABLES*, 1920)

BOTANICALLY, the only thing spinach and chard have in common is their edible and interesting, dark green leaves. Chard leaves, in particular, are very beautiful, large and ruffled, with broad, thick, creamy white ribs. A variety called rhubarb or ruby chard is even more photogenic with its bright red ribs. Chard is related to beetroot (beet) but is cultivated for its leaves rather than for its root. The Italian word for chard is *bietola* and in English, for reasons not clear, it is called Swiss chard. Its scientific name, *cicla*, derives from the Latin word for Sicily, the island with which it was first associated. It has always been a popular green in Mediterranean countries, but I don't recall having ever seen it in markets or on menus outside the area, with the exception of California, which now grows practically everything we have here.

One delicious and interesting dish featuring chard that thoroughly savours of the Mediterranean comes immediately to mind. It is called *seppie in zimino* and consists of cuttlefish stewed with Swiss chard, olive oil, red wine, onion, garlic and chilli pepper. Old Sicilian recipes added cinnamon, saffron and raisons, evidence of ancient Arab influences on the island.

Spinach is similar to chard in taste and can be used as a substitute in most recipes.

The Arabs referred to spinach as the "prince of vegetables". It originated in its wild state in Persia and sometime in the early Middle Ages Arab traders brought it to Sicily and then into Italy, where one thousand years later it still reigns as the most popular cooking green. It can be found somewhere on the peninsula all year round, although it is best in spring and autumn. In many food shops you can buy fresh spinach, as well as chard, chicory and other leafy greens, already cooked and pressed into balls the size of a tennis ball and heat it up at home. I often use it this way to prepare *spinaci saltati*, literally "jumped" spinach, stir-fried in extra-virgin olive oil, seasoned with garlic and, if you like, chilli pepper.

An important attribute of spinach is its versatility in combining with other ingredients, especially in pasta and pastry, with eggs and milk products and spices of all kinds. If you ask a Tuscan about spinach, the first dish that would come to mind are *tortelli*, large ravioli stuffed with spinach and sheep's milk ricotta, sautéed in butter and sage and sprinkled generously with Parmesan.

CHARD WITH RAISINS
Bietole all'uvetta

1KG/2¼LB CHARD
1 ONION, CHOPPED
3 TBSP EXTRA-VIRGIN OLIVE OIL
PINCH OF HOT CHILLI, CRUSHED
300G/10OZ CANNED PLUM TOMATOES,
CHOPPED
1 HANDFUL DARK RAISINS, SOAKED IN
WATER AND DRAINED
SALT

Discard most of the green part of the chard, leaving only the large white stalks (use the leaves for a soup or other recipe). Cut the stalks into 5cm/2in pieces and blanch in boiling water for 1 minute, then drain and reserve. Fry the onion in the oil for about 2 minutes until translucent, then add the chard and the chilli and stir for about 3 minutes. Add the tomatoes with their juice and salt to taste and cover. Lower the heat to minimum and simmer for about 30 minutes, or until the liquid has completely reduced. Add the raisins, stir, arrange on a platter and serve immediately.

Serves 6

SPINACH MOULD
SFORMATO DI SPINACI

1KG/2¼LB SPINACH, WELL WASHED
AND DRAINED
25G/1OZ/2 TBSP UNSALTED BUTTER
4 TBSP PLAIN (ALL-PURPOSE) FLOUR
300ML/10FL OZ/1¼ CUPS MILK
6 TBSP FRESHLY GRATED
PARMESAN CHEESE
3 LARGE EGGS
LARGE PINCH OF GRATED NUTMEG
SALT

Preheat the oven to 180°C/375°F/gas mark 4.

Cook the spinach with their stems in a little boiling, salted water for about 3 minutes until wilted. Drain, squeeze dry and chop very finely – do not process in a blender. To make the sauce, melt the butter in a pan over a medium heat, then add the flour and mix with a wooden spoon until well combined. Add the milk a little at a time and mix well until a dense, smooth sauce is formed. Take the pan off the heat, add the cheese, mix well and let cool. When cooled, add the eggs and nutmeg and pour into a 1 litre/1¾ pint/4 cup, non-stick mould. Place the mould in a baking tray and pour water into the tray to come about 2.5cm/1in up the sides of the mould. Cook for about 50 minutes or until very firm. Let it cool slightly to set, then invert the mould on to a platter and serve.

Serves 6

SPINACH WITH YOGURT
SPINACI ALLO YOGURT

1KG/2¼LB SPINACH, WELL WASHED AND DRAINED
40G/1½OZ/3 TBSP UNSALTED BUTTER
120ML/4FL OZ/½ CUP YOGURT
3 TBSP DARK RAISINS, SOAKED IN WATER FOR ABOUT 30 MINUTES
SALT

Cook the spinach with their stems in a little boiling, salted water for about 3 minutes until wilted. Drain and squeeze dry. Melt the butter in a pan, add the spinach and sauté over a low heat for a few minutes. Add the yogurt, increase the heat and cook for about 3 minutes more. Drain then mix in the raisins and check the salt. Arrange on a platter and serve.

Serves 6

CELERY

(APIUM GRAVEOLENS DULCE)

SINCE WILD CELERY, especially its leaves, has a strong, herbaceous taste (it is from the same family as parsley), its first culinary use was as a flavour base or seasoning and dates from the seventeenth century. Prior to that it seems to have been used for medicinal purposes only, usually as a cure for various digestive problems as well as adding its name to the long list of traditional aphrodisiacs. As celery began to be cultivated, in particular for its bunch of succulent stalks or stems, milder varieties were developed. Today the most common are white and green. White celery is milder and more tender and used raw, while green is cooked.

One of the best ways I know to enjoy the taste of raw celery, fresh and crisp, is as part of a *pinzimonio*. Prepare small, individual bowls of fine extra-virgin olive oil, salt and pepper for your guests as a dip for sliced celery stalks and other raw vegetables. This is a popular summer luncheon antipasto. Raw celery is also part of the traditional cold weather *bagna cauda*. As a dip or a spread, I particularly like the combination of raw celery with creamy, blue-veined Gorgonzola cheese.

Cooked celery is common enough on the table of Italian families, although not so frequently found on restaurant menus. A winter favourite is hearty celery soup with onions and potatoes, and in summer celery purée enriched with cream. Many home cooks braise celery in the juices of their Sunday roast and dress it with Parmesan cheese.

Celery, as a seasoning, is fundamental to innumerable Italian dishes. The point of departure for my cooking classes is teaching the participants to make a *soffritto*.

So basic is it that many recipes written in Italian take it for granted, and begin simply by telling you what to add once the *soffritto* is ready. Celery and onion are its two main ingredients, to which are sometimes added carrot, garlic and parsley, all finely chopped and gently sautéed in olive oil. Literally *soffritto* means to under-fry.

Besides leafy celery, another variety of the same plant is celery root or celeriac, in Italian, *sedano rapa*, cultivated for its sweet and mild, fleshy root, about the size of a small turnip (see p.122 Roots & Bulbs).

CELERY PUREE
PUREA DI SEDANO

1 HEAD OF CELERY, TRIMMED
1KG/2¼LB BOILING POTATOES,
UNPEELED
240ML/8FL OZ/1 CUP MILK
90G/3OZ/6 TBSP UNSALTED BUTTER
SALT

Detach the celery stalks and cut them into pieces. Wash the potatoes, place in a saucepan and well cover with water. Bring the potatoes to the boil, add the celery after 15 minutes and cook until the potatoes are tender. Drain. Peel the potatoes then purée them with the celery through a ricer. Add the milk and butter to the purée, a little at a time. Cook over a low heat, stirring well, for a few minutes, add salt to taste and serve. If you want a softer purée add a little more milk, and for a firmer purée cook a little longer until it reaches the desired consistency.

Serves 6

CELERY CREAM WITH CORIANDER
CREMA DI SEDANO AL CORIANDOLO

1 HEAD OF CELERY, TRIMMED
2 LITRE/3½ PINT/8 CUPS VEGETABLE STOCK
1½ HANDFULS RICE (ANY QUALITY)
240ML/8FL OZ/1 CUP SINGLE (LIGHT) CREAM
1 TBSP CORIANDER SEEDS
6 TBSP EXTRA-VIRGIN OLIVE OIL
SALT AND PEPPER

Detach the celery stalks and cut them into pieces. In a large saucepan, bring the stock to the boil, add the celery, rice and a little salt and cook for about 30 minutes, until very soft.

Drain, reserving the liquid, and pass everything through a food mill. Add the vegetable purée to the reserved liquid with the cream and coriander seeds and cook for 15 minutes more. Check the salt, add pepper to taste and pour into individual soup bowls. Pour 1 tablespoon of oil into each bowl and serve immediately.

Serves 6

CELERY WITH GORGONZOLA CHEESE DIP
SEDANO AL PINZIMONIO DI GORGONZOLA

1 HEAD OF VERY WHITE CELERY, TRIMMED
120G/4OZ GORGONZOLA CHEESE
1 TBSP LEMON JUICE
240ML/8FL OZ/1 CUP EXTRA-VIRGIN OLIVE OIL
SALT AND PEPPER

Detach the celery stalks and put them in a bowl with a little water and a few ice cubes, to keep the celery crisp. Blend the Gorgonzola cheese with the lemon juice, then add the oil a little at a time, to obtain a fluid cream. Pour the cream into 6 individual small bowls, and add a little salt and pepper to taste. Serve the celery with the dip, coating the stems with the cream before every bite.

Serves 6

CARDOONS

(CYNARA CARDUNCULUS)

I HAVE NOTICED in my travels that cardoons, *cardi* in Italian, are not well known outside the Mediterranean region where they were first cultivated and still grow wild. The cardoon is an edible thistle, like the artichoke to which it is closely related. It grows several feet high and has long spiny leaves along the stalk, which blossoms in a large and splendid purplish-blue flower, adding its glorious colour to the wild spring and summer flowers that adorn the Mediterranean landscape.

Cardoons are cultivated for their tender stalk, which has a mild, herbaceous flavour, reminiscent of the artichoke. They bring back happy memories of my childhood, when I frequently spent weekends and holidays with my cousins in Piedmont. Our favourite meal was *bagna cauda*, which in the dialect of that region means "hot bath". The bath is a pot of hot butter and olive oil to which is added finely chopped garlic cloves and anchovy fillets that are cooked until dissolved and then kept warm in an earthenware chafing dish placed in the centre of the table. Everyone dips pieces of cardoons and an assortment of other suitable raw vegetables, such as slices of sweet peppers, carrot sticks, and celery, into the pot. *Bagna cauda* is a perfect dish for a gathering of family and friends. The communal effort keeps the children happy and engenders sociability among the adults, as does the traditional abundance of red wine to wash the meal down. What I did not realize at the time was that after the children had been excused from table, if it was the right season, my aunt would shave a precious white truffle, another delicacy of the region, into the remains of the sauce and the adults would wipe the pot clean with slices of country bread.

In Tuscany we eat cardoons stewed, usually with tomato sauce or baked with butter and Parmesan cheese. Makers of pecorino toscano, sheep's milk cheese, traditionally use the dried flowers of cardoons as a rennet. Someone many centuries ago discovered that the enzymes found on the stamens of the flower curdle milk. Local cheese makers claim it also adds to the pleasant herbal flavour of their product – that and the sweet green pasture of the Tuscany countryside.

CARDOONS IN OIL AND BUTTER DIP
CARDI IN BAGNA CAUDA

1 CARDOON

JUICE OF 1 LEMON

120G/4OZ/8 TBSP UNSALTED BUTTER

120ML/4FL OZ/½ CUP EXTRA-VIRGIN OLIVE OIL

3 ANCHOVY FILLETS IN OIL, DRAINED

3 GARLIC CLOVES, CHOPPED

SALT AND PEPPER

Strip off and discard the base, leaves and spiny outer stalks of the cardoon. Detach the stalks and trim the ends. Immerse the stalks in a large bowl of water acidulated with the lemon juice. Heat the butter and oil in a terracotta pot, arranged over a chafing dish in the middle of the table, add the anchovies and mash them with a fork, until dissolved. Add the garlic and keep the flame low. Drain the cardoon stalks and pat dry. Each person should get a stalk, immerse it in the frying oil and cook for a couple of minutes.

Serves 6

CARDOONS WITH MEAT RAGU
CARDI AL RAGÚ DI CARNE

1 CARDOON

JUICE OF 1 LEMON

2 TBSP EXTRA-VIRGIN OLIVE OIL

1 TBSP UNSALTED BUTTER

1 GARLIC CLOVE, CHOPPED

1 TBSP CHOPPED FLAT-LEAF

ITALIAN PARSLEY

120G/4OZ MINCED MEAT

120G/4OZ CHOPPED SWEET

ITALIAN SAUSAGES

300G/10OZ CANNED PLUM TOMATOES,

CHOPPED

SALT AND PEPPER

Strip off and discard the base, leaves and spiny outer stalks of the cardoon. Cut the remaining stalks into pieces about 9cm/3in long. Immerse them in a large bowl of water acidulated with the lemon juice.

Heat the oil and butter in a large saucepan, add the garlic and cook for about 2 minutes until translucent. Add the parsley, chopped meat and sausage and cook, stirring occasionally, for about 5 minutes, until golden. Add the tomatoes with their juice and salt and pepper. Cover the pan and cook for about 1 hour over a low heat, adding more water if necessary to keep the cooking juices moist. Add the cardoons, cover again and cook for about 10 minutes more, or until tender. Check the seasoning, arrange on a platter and serve.

Serves 6

CARDOONS FRIED IN BREADCRUMBS

CARDI IN COSTOLETTA

1 CARDOON

JUICE OF 1 LEMON

1 LARGE EGG, BEATEN

180G/6OZ/1½ CUPS DRIED FINE BREADCRUMBS

60G/2OZ/4 TBSP UNSALTED BUTTER

4 TBSP EXTRA-VIRGIN OLIVE OIL

SALT AND PEPPER

Strip off and discard the base, leaves and spiny outer stalks of the cardoon. Detach the stalks and cut them into pieces about 9cm/3in long and immerse them in a large bowl of water acidulated with the lemon juice. Beat the egg with salt and pepper in a deep dish. Drain the cardoons and pat dry then coat them in the beaten egg, and roll them in the breadcrumbs to coat well. Heat the butter and oil in a non-stick pan, add the cardoons and cook over a low heat for a few minutes, turning them once, until golden and barely tender. Drain on a paper towel and serve immediately.

Serves 6

KOHLRABI

(BRASSICA OLERACEA CAULORAPA)

A STRANGE NAME FOR A strange vegetable, Kohlrabi belongs to the extensive cabbage family, *Brassica oleracea*. Its name derives from the German for cabbage, *kohl*, and the Latin for turnip, *rapa*, another member of *Brassica*. An 18th-century German botanist erroneously thought it was a cross between a cabbage and turnip and its Italian name, *cavolo rapa*, is a literal translation of the same misconception.

It is easy to see how kohlrabi got its mistaken identity. It has a root-like globe not unlike a turnip and leaves similar to cabbage greens, but smaller. The globe, however, is really the swollen base of the green stems and grows partially above ground. There are two principal varieties, white and purple. I find the flavour of both more reminiscent of cauliflower, another member of *Brassica oleracea*, than turnip.

Kohlrabi is a novelty to most Italians, except those who live on the northern borders – I first tasted it in Trieste. I was surprised that the 17th-century writer on Italian fruits and vegetables Giacomo Castelvetro even mentions it. At the conclusion of his discourse on cabbages, he says, "the leaves are quite nice, but the so-called root…is absolutely delicious". He suggests that it be cooked in a rich broth and served seasoned with grated cheese, salt, pepper and spices.

If it is fresh from the garden, cook the leaves with the globe for flavour or on their own, as you would spinach or turnip tops. Buy kohlrabi when it is still small, about the size of an orange. Larger ones will be too tough to bother with.

KOHLRABI WITH ANCHOVIES

Cavolo rapa all'acciuga

1kg/2¼lb kohlrabi
6 tbsp extra-virgin olive oil
4 anchovy fillets in oil, drained
90g/3oz/½ cup dried fine
breadcrumbs
4 garlic cloves, minced
salt and pepper

Bring a large saucepan of salted water to the boil. Peel the kohlrabi and slice thinly. Cook in the water for about 5 minutes and then drain. Place the oil in a saucepan over a low heat. Add the anchovies with the oil, breadcrumbs and the garlic, and sauté for about 3 minutes, stirring constantly. Reserve half the mixture and then add the kohlrabi to the pan. Add a little water, cover and cook for 5 minutes more, until tender. Add the pepper, arrange on a platter, cover with the remaining breadcrumb mixture and serve immediately.

Serves 6

KOHLRABI WITH CREAM

Cavolo rapa alla panna

1kg/2¼lb kohlrabi
240ml/8fl oz/1 cup double (heavy)
cream
2 tbsp chopped flat-leaf Italian
parsley
salt and pepper

Bring a large saucepan of salted water to the boil. Peel the kohlrabi and cut them into julienne strips. Cook in the water for about 5 minutes, then drain and replace in the saucepan. Add the cream and pepper to taste and cover. Cook over a low heat for 5 minutes more, uncover and continue cooking until most of the cream has evaporated. Add the parsley, mix well, arrange on a platter and serve immediately.

Serves 6

KOHLRABI SOUP

Minestra di cavolo rapa

600g/1¼lb kohlrabi
6 tbsp extra-virgin olive oil
1 white onion, chopped
120g/4oz bacon in one piece
1 carrot, chopped
3 garlic cloves, chopped
2 large potatoes, diced
salt and pepper

Peel the kohlrabi and dice. Heat 3 tablespoons of the oil in a saucepan, add the onion and bacon and cook over a low heat for about 3 minutes until translucent, stirring continuously. Add the kohlrabi, carrot, garlic, potatoes and about 2 litres/3½ pints/8 cups of water and bring to the boil. Cook with the lid on for about 1 hour. Discard the bacon and add salt and pepper to taste. Pour into a soup tureen, add the remaining oil and serve immediately.

Serves 6

ARTICHOKES

(CYNARA SCOLYMUS)

I F I HAD TO NAME the Italian vegetable *per eccellenza*, it would be the *carciofo*, the globe artichoke. This member of the thistle family, related to the wild cardoon, is probably native to the Mediterranean region of North Africa but it is thanks to Italian gardeners and cooks that the plant was developed to its full and delicious potential. Today Italy is the world's largest producer and consumer of artichokes.

Artichokes are cultivated for their flower head, picked before it blossoms. Dozens of varieties are grown along the peninsula. In late March and early April in the markets of Venice you see tiny *castraure*. Their name, *castrates*, is appropriate. These tiny balls are the lateral bud of the artichoke plant that has to be cut off so that the main buds can develop. Each plant has only one. Unenlightened gardeners throw them away. Venetians eat them. They are tender and delicious beyond description. In Tuscan markets, early spring arrivals are the *violetti di toscana*, "Tuscan violets", so-called because of their purple petal-like leaves, called bracts. When their bud is still small, the bracts can be eaten raw, dressed with extra-virgin olive oil and a little salt. The most common artichoke is the globe-shaped variety developed by the ancient Romans called *Romanesco*. Contemporary Romans trim away all its tough parts and braise it whole, together with its tender stem, in a mixture of olive oil, parsley, garlic and mint. These *carciofi alla romana* are most often served warm or at room temperature as an antipasto. A speciality of Roman–Jewish cuisine is *carciofi alla Giudia*, globe artichokes deep-fried in such a way that the outer leaves are crisp and the centre tender.

Unlike roses, there are artichokes without thorns but all except the tiny spring variety have to be liberated from their tough outer leaves, often up to a quarter of the bud, until you can enjoy the pale, edible bracts enclosing the succulent heart. Cleaning, however, is no big deal and only requires a sharp paring knife and/or willing fingers and patience. Don't forget to drop the artichokes into some water acidulated with the juice of a lemon as you go along, to prevent them from discolouring. In Italy you can usually find artichokes on sale at farmers' markets already cleaned for you – yet another Italian contribution to the civilization of the artichoke.

ARTICHOKES WITH PARSLEY AND GARLIC

CARCIOFI ALLA ROMANA

6 ARTICHOKES

JUICE OF 1 LEMON

3 GARLIC CLOVES, CHOPPED

2 TBSP FLAT-LEAF ITALIAN PARSLEY, CHOPPED

3 TBSP EXTRA-VIRGIN OLIVE OIL

SALT AND PEPPER

Trim the artichokes and discard the tough outer leaves, the stems and the furry chokes (if any). Drop them into a bowl of water acidulated with the lemon juice, to prevent discolouration. Drain, open the leaves slightly and fill with the garlic, parsley, a little salt and pepper and 1 tablespoon of the oil. Pour the remaining oil into a deep saucepan and arrange the artichokes tightly together in one layer in the pan. Pour in a couple of tablespoons of water, cover with a lid and cook over a low heat for about 15 minutes, adding more water if necessary to keep the cooking juices moist. Arrange the artichokes on a platter and serve.

Serves 6

JEWISH-STYLE ARTICHOKES
CARCIOFI ALLA GIUDEA

6 ARTICHOKES
JUICE OF 1 LEMON
1 LITRE/1¾ PINT/4 CUPS OIL
FOR DEEP-FRYING
SALT AND PEPPER

Trim the artichokes and discard the tough outer leaves, the stems and furry chokes (if any). Drop them into a bowl of water acidulated with the lemon juice, to prevent discolouration. Drain and pat dry. Using the heel of your hand, press down on the centre of each artichoke to flatten the leaves a little. Heat the oil to 150°C/300°F in a deep frying pan. Place the artichokes in the pan, lower the heat slightly, and cook for about 5 minutes. Turn them and cook for 2 minutes more. Drain on a paper towel, sprinkle with salt and pepper and serve immediately.

Serves 6

ARTICHOKE AND PARMESAN CHEESE SALAD
INSALATA DI CARCIOFI E GRANA

6 YOUNG ARTICHOKES WITH THORNS
JUICE OF 1 LEMON
4 TBSP EXTRA-VIRGIN OLIVE OIL
120G/4OZ PIECE PARMESAN CHEESE
SALT AND PEPPER

Trim the artichokes and discard the tough outer leaves, the stems and the furry chokes (if any). Quarter them lengthwise. Drop them into a bowl of water acidulated with the lemon juice, to prevent discolouration. Drain and pat dry. Slice them thinly lengthwise and arrange on a platter. Sprinkle with salt and pepper and the oil and shave the Parmesan cheese on top. Serve immediately.

Serves 6

CHICORY

(CICHORIUM INTYBUS)

Both as a gardener and as a cook I think of chicory in the plural. Cultivated since the sixteenth century, there are so many chicories of various shapes and colours that it often leads to confusion.

Radicchio, in both its red and green varieties, is particularly popular in Italy, though the appeal of its bitter flavour is widely spreading. *Radicchio di Treviso*, *radicchio di Castelfranco* and *rossa di Verona* are the main types of red radicchio, while the loose-leafed green variety is one of spring's tastiest salad greens. It comes to market in a tight bunch with the stems all together. It is sliced paper thin, often using scissors, which renders it less bitter. My greengrocer in Tuscany sells it with a stalk of young, green garlic hidden in the bunch, its perfect culinary complement.

Escarole, French endive, Belgian endive and curly endive are also chicories, as is the dandelion, an edible weed similar to wild chicory. Endive, is an excellent green. Its various types are slightly less bitter than other chicories, which makes it suitable for salads, and have the same substantial and crunchy texture, which makes them good for cooking as well. Endive combines perfectly with rich tastes, sharp and strong cheese, with flavours such as anchovy and garlic, and braised with tomato and meat sauce.

In Italy and other parts of southern Europe during the war years, the chicory root was ground as a substitute for coffee, which was scarce and prohibitively expensive. I remember friends of my parents who, long after the war was over, preferred a little chicory mixed with their coffee.

CHICORY AND BROAD BEAN SOUP
Minestra di cicoria con le fave

300G/10OZ DRIED BROAD BEANS
1 LARGE WHITE ONION, SLICED
6 GARLIC CLOVES, SLICED
600G/1¼LB CATALOGNA CHICORY
OR ESCAROLE
PINCH OF CHILLI POWDER
6 TBSP EXTRA-VIRGIN OLIVE OIL
SALT

Put the beans in a bowl, cover with water and soak overnight. Drain the beans and place in a saucepan with the onion, garlic, salt to taste and 2 litres/3½ pints/8 cups water. Bring to a slow boil and cook for about 1 hour. Wash the chicory and slice roughly. Add to the saucepan and cook for 10 minutes more. Pour into a soup tureen, add the chilli and the oil and serve.

Serves 6

CHICORY AND TOMATO SALAD
Insalata di cicoria e pomodori

1 GARLIC CLOVE
300G/10OZ SPADONA CHICORY OR
YOUNG SPINACH LEAVES
3 RIPE SALAD TOMATOES, SLICED
1 TBSP RED WINE VINEGAR
4 TBSP EXTRA-VIRGIN OLIVE OIL
SALT AND PEPPER

Rub the garlic clove around the inside of a salad bowl, pressing lightly, and discard.

Wash the chicory, spin dry and arrange in a tight bunch with all the stems together. Using a knife or with scissors, slice the chicory paper thin and arrange in the salad bowl. Arrange the tomatoes around the chicory. Dissolve a little salt with the vinegar, add the oil and mix well to blend. Pour over the salad and serve immediately.

Serves 6

BELGIAN ENDIVE WITH ALMONDS
Indivia del Belgio alle mandorle

12 BELGIAN ENDIVES
JUICE OF 1 LEMON
90G/3OZ/6 TBSP UNSALTED BUTTER
3 LARGE EGGS
240ML/8FL OZ/1 CUP DOUBLE
(HEAVY) CREAM
6 TBSP FRESHLY GRATED
PARMESAN CHEESE
120G/4OZ ALMONDS, TOASTED
AND CHOPPED
SALT AND PEPPER

Preheat the oven to 200°C/400°F/gas mark 6.

Arrange the endives in a large saucepan, add the lemon juice and 1 tablespoon of the butter. Cover with water, add salt to taste, bring to the boil and cook for 3 minutes. Drain and arrange on a heatproof dish. Beat the egg yolks in a bowl, add the cream, Parmesan cheese and salt to taste and mix well. Pour over the endives and cook for about 20 minutes in the oven, or until the eggs are set. Sprinkle the almonds over the top and cook for 3 minutes more. Sprinkle with pepper and serve, piping hot.

Serves 6

LETTUCES

(LACTUCA)

"Lettuce, like conversation, requires a good deal of oil, to avoid friction, and keep the company smooth."

(Charles Dudley Warner, "Ninth Week", *My Summer in a Garden*, 1871)

Over the centuries Italians from various regions of the peninsula have been given nicknames by their fellow countrymen based on the particular region's favoured food. In a teasing sort of way, Tuscans are called *mangiafagioli*, bean-eaters, and the inhabitants of Naples, *mangiafoglie*, leaf-eaters. About four centuries ago my ancestors left Florence for what was then the Kingdom of Naples, where they settled for several centuries before going up to the northern region of Piedmont. Like my Neapolitan forebears I, however, remain a leaf-eater. Greens of all kinds, both wild and domestic, are my favourite food. And a simple salad from my garden, composed of tasty leafy lettuces tossed with a dressing of extra-virgin olive oil and red wine vinegar, is my favourite dish.

The Italian name for mixed salad greens is *misticanza*, like the Provençal, *mesclun*.

In some regions *misticanza* refers only to a mixture of wild greens, for others it means a mixture of cultivated, little salad greens. The secrets of a good *misticanza* are two – a balanced combination of flavours and a simple dressing of fine extra-virgin olive oil and good quality red wine vinegar. In his informative book, *Brieve racconto di tutte le radici, di tutte l'herbe et di tutti i frutti, che crudi o cotti in Italia si mangiano*, translated as the "Fruits, Herbs and Vegetables of Italy", written in 1614, Giacomo Castelvetro gives this recipe for *misticanza*, as refreshing today as it was almost four hundred years ago: "Of all the salads we eat in the spring, the mixed salad is the best and the most wonderful of all. Take young leaves of mint, garden cress, basil, lemon balm, the tips of salad burnet, tarragon, the flowers and the most tender leaves of borage, the flowers of swine cress, the young shoots of fennel, leaves of rocket, of sorrel, rosemary flowers, some sweet violets, and the most tender leaves or the hearts of lettuce. When these precious herbs have been picked clean and washed several times, and dried a little with a clean linen cloth, they are dressed as usual, with oil, salt and vinegar."

Part of the chicory family (see p.52), the popular, loose-leaf *radicchio di Treviso* is rather like a small romaine lettuce, with purple-red tapered leaves that have creamy white ribs. Sometimes the effect is almost like an elongated parrot tulip. It has a pleasingly bitter taste, which I enjoy both raw and cooked. Its extremely complicated process of forced cultivation makes it expensive as well as short-seasoned.

FILLED LETTUCE

Lattughe ripiene

6 ROUND LETTUCE HEADS
6 HANDFULS SOFT FRESH
BREADCRUMBS, SOAKED IN MILK AND
SQUEEZED DRY
120G/4OZ/¾ CUP FRESHLY GRATED
PARMESAN CHEESE
150G/5OZ COOKED HAM,
FINELY CHOPPED
3 LARGE EGG YOLKS
3 TBSP EXTRA-VIRGIN OLIVE OIL
SALT AND PEPPER

Bring a large saucepan of salted water to the boil. Trim the lettuces, discarding some outer leaves, and blanch them for 30 seconds in the boiling water. Drain and pat dry. In a bowl, mix the breadcrumbs with the cheese and the cooked ham, add the egg yolks and blend well. Add pepper to taste. Carefully open each lettuce and fill the centre with the mixture then fold in the leaves in order to enclose the filling. Pour the oil into a large saucepan, add a little water and place the lettuces in the pan. Cover with a lid and cook for about 10 minutes, over a low heat, turning them carefully once. Add more water, if necessary, to keep the cooking juices moist. Arrange on a platter and serve.

Serves 6

LETTUCE WITH GORGONZOLA AND WALNUTS

Lattuga con gorgonzola e noci

300G/10OZ COS LETTUCE, WASHED AND DRIED
180G/6OZ GORGONZOLA CHEESE, CRUMBLED
1 TBSP RED WINE VINEGAR
PINCH POWDERED MUSTARD
1 LARGE EGG YOLK
4 TBSP EXTRA-VIRGIN OLIVE OIL
90G/3OZ SHELLED AND CHOPPED WALNUTS
SALT

Slice the cos lettuce thinly and arrange in a salad bowl. Sprinkle the Gorgonzola on top. Dissolve a little salt to taste with the vinegar, add the mustard and the egg yolk and mix well. Add the oil and stir to blend. Pour over the salad and toss. Sprinkle with the walnuts and serve at room temperature.

Serves 6

GRILLED RADICCHIO WITH ANCHOVIES

RADICCHIO ALLA GRIGLIA CON ACCIUGA

1KG/2¼LB RED RADICCHIO, ROOTS
REMOVED
6 TBSP EXTRA-VIRGIN OLIVE OIL
6 ANCHOVY FILLETS IN OIL, DRAINED
1 GARLIC CLOVE, MASHED
1 TBSP BALSAMIC VINEGAR
SALT AND PEPPER

Clean the radicchio and cut into quarters. Brush a pan with a little oil, arrange the radicchio in the pan, cover and cook until wilted, about 5 minutes, turning it several times. In a small bowl, mash the anchovies with a fork, add the garlic, oil, balsamic vinegar and salt and pepper to taste and mix well. Arrange the radicchio on a platter, pour the sauce over and serve warm or at room temperature.

Serves 6

CRESS & WATERCRESS

(LEPIDUM, CARDAMINE, ARABIS/RORIPPA NASTURTIUM-AQUATICUM)

CRESS, WATERCRESS, ROCKET AND DANDELION leaves make up a curious bouquet, yet they do have a culinary common denominator – their very distinct taste, which is variously described as spicy, nutty and peppery. For many, but not for all, palates their assertive flavour is a welcome addition when they are tossed together with blander greens.

Many types of cress grow both wild and cultivated. They are all members of the mustard family. A friend who lives in a medieval mill house down the hill from my home in Tuscany keeps me supplied in spring with watercress, the most popular of the species. It grows in abundance along his millstream, where conditions are ideal – cool temperatures and a steady supply of fresh water. I find it has to be used very soon after picking, otherwise it turns unpleasantly bitter. Its lovely, small, bright green leaves and tiny stems make a perfect garnish for all meat and fish dishes. Watercress has a pleasant crunch to the bite. I can't have enough of it in green salads and it is very tasty in fruit salads, combined with oranges or apples or pears. Garden cress is much the same as watercress, perhaps a bit more tender with more pepper in the flavour. I have tried making cress soup, using the same recipe for other green vegetable soups. It is delightful served chilled for a summer supper.

I can remember when rocket (arugula) took off like a rocket in the United States. It must have been in the early seventies. It was all the rage and cost a fortune. I hesitated to tell my American friends who were restaurant cooks that it grew like a weed in my garden. Now I'm sure it does in theirs. There are two kinds of arugula, or as it is more commonly called in Italy, rucola or rughetta (*Eruca sativa*, in Latin, rocket in English, roquette in French) the wild plant that has a thinner leaf and thicker stem and is considerably more peppery, and the cultivated variety, which is wider leafed and milder in flavour. Use young and tender rocket in salads – I enjoy it most with cherry tomatoes. Try wilting more mature and peppery rocket with warm potatoes, dressed with olive oil, salt and pepper. Its flavour also combines well with cheese.

Dandelion greens are still wildly popular with the older generation of Italian foragers. Out in the country you often see grandmothers with their grandchildren walking through the fields picking them as they go along. Botanically the dandelion, whose name is derived from the French, meaning lion's teeth, because of its serrated leaf, is a chicory and can be used in the same way. Dandelions are also cultivated and are less bitter than the wild variety, which has to be eaten while still very young. A traditional way to cook dandelion greens is to sauté them with *pancetta* or lardons.

ROCKET WITH GOAT CHEESE
RUCOLA CON FORMAGGIO DI CAPRA

300G/10OZ ROCKET (ARUGULA)
2 LARGE RIPE SALAD TOMATOES,
SLICED
2 SPRING ONIONS (SCALLIONS), SLICED
3 RADISHES, SLICED
1 TBSP BALSAMIC VINEGAR
4 TBSP EXTRA-VIRGIN OLIVE OIL
SALT

Clean the rocket (arugula), discarding any tough stems, and arrange with the tomatoes, onions and radishes on a salad platter. Dissolve the salt with the balsamic vinegar, add the oil and pour over the salad. Toss before serving at room temperature.

Serves 4

CRESS OR WATERCRESS WITH SOJA
CRESCIONE ALLA SOIA

300G/10OZ CRESS OR WATERCRESS
90G/3OZ SOJA SPROUTS
60G/2OZ PISTACHIOS, SHELLED
1 TBSP SOJA SAUCE
PINCH OF SUGAR
3 TBSP EXTRA-VIRGIN OLIVE OIL
SALT

Wash and clean the cress or watercress and the soja sprouts. Arrange them in a salad bowl, add the pistachios and mix. Toss the salad with the soja sauce, sugar, oil and salt to taste and serve at room temperature.

Serves 6

DANDELION SAUTEED WITH GARLIC
TARASSACO ALL'AGLIO

600G/1¼LB DANDELION LEAVES
3 HEADS OF GARLIC, UNPEELED
3 TBSP EXTRA-VIRGIN OLIVE OIL
SALT

Preheat the oven to 170°C/350°F/gas mark 3.

Clean the dandelion leaves, and chop off and discard any roots. Bring a large saucepan of water to the boil, add salt and the dandelion leaves and blanch for 1 minute. Drain. Put the garlic heads on a baking tray (cookie sheet) and cook in the oven for about 20 minutes until tender. Squeeze out the pulp from the cloves, one at a time, into a bowl and mix with the oil and a little salt. Heat in a pan over a low heat with a drop of water, then add the dandelion leaves and cook for about 10 minutes, stirring a couple of times. Arrange on a platter and serve.

Serves 6

LEGUMES

PEAS

(PISUM SATIVUM)

OF ALL THE GIFTS growing in my kitchen garden, come late spring the one I take most pleasure in is peas, small, plump, bright green, sweet and tender. Eating freshly picked peas right off the vine is a gastronomic experience I would rate at the very top of the scale. They really do not even have to be cooked. At the most I blanch them for a couple of minutes and dress with a little extra-virgin olive oil, salt and pepper. After that first pristine tasting of the season, at other times I season them with sautéed onion and a little bouquet of chopped mint leaves.

The ancestor of today's garden pea is one of the oldest vegetables known. Originating in western Asia, peas were much prized by primitive man as well as by ancient Greeks and Romans, as they could be dried and provide nourishment throughout the year. In those days they were eaten in their pod. Peas as we now enjoy them were first cultivated in Europe in the sixteenth century, and were much the fashion in royal gardens and on regal tables. Caterina de'Medici is said to have favoured them in France, where they are picked very young and served as *petit pois*. The pea has remained a staple in the diet of many countries, probably because it

freezes so well. Forget processed peas in a can. They are so far removed from the real thing as to constitute another food.

Perhaps the most traditional Italian recipe for peas is cooked with pieces of *prosciutto*, Parma ham, and extra-virgin olive oil. These same ingredients make a delicious pasta sauce. The most renowned Venetian dish with peas is called, in dialect, *risi e bisi*. Depending on your point of view, it could either be seen as a thick rice soup or as an excessively runny risotto. Whichever way you think of it, *risi e bisi* with the season's first peas is culinary perfection.

Besides the garden pea in its pod, which must be shucked, there is another variety with flat, light green, edible pods through which you can just make out the shape of the tiny peas inside. These are called sugar peas or, more descriptively in French, *mangetout*, because you can eat the whole thing. Sugar snaps and Chinese snow peas are of this type. These varieties, however, have never been popular in Italy, where they are called *taccole*, except for animal feed. Years ago I brought back snow pea seeds from a trip to California and planted them in my garden in Tuscany where, I am happy to report, they thrive.

GARDEN PEAS WITH FENNEL
PISELLI ALL'ANETO

2KG/4½LB FRESH GARDEN PEAS,
SHELLED AND PODS DISCARDED
1 SMALL WHITE ONION, CHOPPED
6 TBSP EXTRA-VIRGIN OLIVE OIL
1 TBSP FRESH FENNEL FRONDS
(ANETH), CHOPPED
SALT AND PEPPER

Bring a large saucepan of water to the boil, add some salt and the peas. Blanch for 1 minute, then drain and rinse under cold water to retain their colour. Set aside. Fry the onion in half of the oil over a low heat until translucent. Add the peas and mix gently, then cover and cook for about 3 minutes, or less if the peas are really small. Sprinkle with the fennel, a little pepper and the remaining oil. Mix well, arrange on a platter and serve immediately.

Serves 6

PEA SAUCE
FOR PASTA OR RICE
SALSA DI PISELLI PER PASTA O RISO

1KG/2¼LB GARDEN PEAS, SHELLED AND
PODS DISCARDED
175ML/6FL OZ/¾ CUP EXTRA-VIRGIN
OLIVE OIL
FEW FRESH CHIVES
1 HANDFUL FRESH TARRAGON LEAVES
1 HANDFUL PINENUTS
SALT AND PEPPER

Cook the peas in boiling, salted water for 5 minutes. Drain, reserving 120ml/ 4fl oz/½ cup of the cooking water. Rinse the peas under cold water to retain their colour. Blend the peas with the oil, chives, tarragon, pinenuts and a little pepper in a blender until creamy. Add the reserved cooking water to dilute the sauce. Reheat in a saucepan and pour over pasta or boiled rice, mixing well.

Serves 6

PEA AND RICE SOUP
Minestra di riso e piselli

1.75 LITRE/3 PINT/6 CUPS LIGHT
CHICKEN STOCK
9 HANDFULS ARBORIO RICE
600G/1¼LB PEAS, SHELLED AND
PODS DISCARDED
2 TBSP FINELY CHOPPED FLAT-LEAF
ITALIAN PARSLEY
SALT AND PEPPER

Bring the stock to the boil, add the rice and cook for 10 minutes. Add the peas and cook for 4 minutes more. Add the parsley and pepper to taste. Check the salt, pour into a soup tureen and serve immediately.

Serves 6

NOODLES WITH SUGAR SNAPS
Tagliatelle alle taccole

480G/1LB SUGAR SNAP PEAS
480G/1LB DRIED FETTUCCINE
2 TBSP EXTRA-VIRGIN OLIVE OIL
360ML/12FL OZ/1½ CUPS DOUBLE (HEAVY) CREAM
120G/4OZ FONTINA CHEESE, GRATED
1 HANDFUL TOASTED HAZELNUTS
SALT AND PEPPER

Trim the tops and tails of the sugar snap peas and remove the strings on the sides. Bring a large saucepan of water to the boil, add a little salt, the noodles and the sugar snap peas. Cook for about 5 minutes, then drain and toss with the oil to prevent the noodles sticking. Meanwhile, boil the cream in a pan for about 5 minutes, add the noodles with the sugar snap peas, and cook, stirring, for a couple of minutes. Arrange on a platter, sprinkle with the fontina cheese, pepper to taste and the hazelnuts and serve immediately.

Serves 6

MANGETOUT WITH SOJA SAUCE
Mangiatutto alla soia

1KG/2¼LB MANGETOUT
6 TBSP EXTRA-VIRGIN OLIVE OIL
3 TBSP SOJA SAUCE
1 TSP CASTER SUGAR

Trim the tops and tails of the mangetout and remove the strings on the sides. Slice them crosswise. Heat the oil in a pan, add the mangetout and cook over a high heat for about 5 minutes, or until tender, stirring continuously. Pour off the oil and add the soja to the pan with 2 tablespoons of water. Stir for a couple of minutes to amalgamate the flavours, then arrange on a platter and serve immediately.

Serves 6

GREEN BEANS

(PHASEOLUS VULGARIS/P. MULTIFLORUS)

EVERY YEAR I ritually celebrate summer's arrival with a platter of young green beans fresh from my garden. I drop them into salted, boiling water for a few minutes, let them cool to room temperature and then dress them with extra-virgin olive oil and lemon. This dish takes the place of salad on my menu for a light alfresco luncheon.

Beans came to Europe from the Americas. Over the centuries gardeners on both continents have developed many varieties. Here I am concerned with green beans, picked while their pods are still edible, tender and sweet, and the seeds inside are tiny. Since the ends of slightly more mature green beans can be snapped off, these became known as snap beans. With age green beans develop tough strings, which have be pulled off before eating, thus the American name, string beans, although this characteristic has been bred-out in modern times. In England green beans are often called French beans, while in France they are *haricots verts*. Their Italian name is *fagiolini*.

Green beans are wonderfully versatile. A delicious way to enjoy them young is par-boiled and then sautéed in olive oil and sprinkled with Parmesan. I often serve them with fish dishes. Fresh green beans should always be cooked *al dente*. As their season progresses, they make the perfect accompaniment to roasts. The traditional Tuscan way to cook mature green beans is stewed in tomato sauce with olive oil and garlic.

One of the most elegant dishes I have ever been served used green beans to encase, one by one, a rich tuna mousse made in a ring mould. I tried re-creating it at home. As it is served cold, you can spend plenty of time arranging the beans. It takes, however, patience and nimble fingers. I decided it was best to keep it as a delicious memory.

70

LINGUINE PASTA WITH GREEN BEANS

LINGUINE COI FAGIOLINI

480G/1LB FRENCH BEANS
480G/1LB LINGUINE
2 HANDFULS BASIL LEAVES
90G/3OZ/⅔ CUP GRATED PECORINO
(ROMANO) CHEESE
120ML/4FL OZ/½ CUP EXTRA-VIRGIN
OLIVE OIL
SALT AND PEPPER

Trim the beans, discarding the tops and tails. Bring a saucepan of water to the boil, add salt and the linguine. Boil for 3 minutes then add the beans and cook for 6 minutes more. Meanwhile, put the basil, a little salt, pepper to taste, the pecorino cheese and the oil into a blender and blend until creamy. Add 90ml/3fl oz/⅜ cup of the cooking water and mix for a few seconds. Drain the pasta and beans and arrange in a bowl. Add the basil and cheese sauce, mix well and serve immediately.

Serves 6

GREEN BEANS WITH ANCHOVY SAUCE

FAGIOLINI ALL'ACCIUGATA

1KG/2¼LB GREEN BEANS
6 TBSP EXTRA-VIRGIN OLIVE OIL
3 GARLIC CLOVES, CHOPPED
2 ANCHOVY FILLETS IN OIL, DRAINED AND CHOPPED
SALT

Trim the beans, discarding the tops and tails. Bring a saucepan of water to the boil, add salt and the beans and cook for about 6 minutes. Drain, then rinse the beans under cold water to keep them green. Heat the oil in a large pan and fry the garlic and anchovies over a low heat, mashing the anchovies with a fork to cream them, for about 3 minutes until translucent. Add the beans, cover and cook for 3 minutes more, stirring occasionally, to blend the flavours. Arrange on a platter and serve immediately.

Serves 6

STEWED RUNNER BEANS

FAGIOLINI DI S. ANNA IN UMIDO

1KG/2¼LB RUNNER BEANS
1 SMALL WHITE ONION, CHOPPED
2 TBSP FLAT-LEAF ITALIAN PARSLEY, CHOPPED
SMALL PIECE OF CELERY STALK, CHOPPED
6 TBSP EXTRA-VIRGIN OLIVE OIL
480G/1LB PLUM TOMATOES, PEELED AND CHOPPED
SALT AND PEPPER

Trim the runner beans and remove the strings on the sides. Slice them crosswise. Fry the onion, parsley and celery in the oil over a low heat for about 3 minutes until translucent. Add the runner beans and sauté over a medium heat for about 2 minutes. Add the tomatoes and salt and pepper to taste, cover and simmer for about 20 minutes, until the cooking liquid has evaporated. Arrange on a platter and serve.

Serves 6

GREEN BEANS WITH PRAWNS
FAGIOLINI AI GAMBERETTI

480G/1LB GREEN BEANS
480G/1LB RAW, SHELLED PRAWNS, HEADS REMOVED
1 TSP LEMON JUICE
6 TBSP EXTRA-VIRGIN OLIVE OIL
1 TBSP CHOPPED FRESH MARJORAM
SALT AND PEPPER

Trim the beans, discarding the tops and tails. Bring a saucepan of water to the boil, add salt and the beans and cook for about 4 minutes. Add the prawns and cook for a couple of minutes more, until they turn pink. Drain and arrange on a platter. Blend the lemon juice with the oil, pour over the beans and mix gently. Sprinkle with the marjoram and serve lukewarm or at room temperature.

Serves 6

BROAD BEANS

(VICIA FABIA)

"*And this is good old Boston,*
The home of the bean and the cod,
Where the Lowells talk to the Cabots,
And the Cabots talk only to God."

(J.C. BOSSIDY 1860–1928, TOAST PROPOSED AT HARVARD DINNER, 1910)

WHY DO I think of broad beans, *fave*, as particularly Italian? After all, they have been around in Europe and most of the rest of the world for centuries, even millenniums. Perhaps it is because, while in most places broad beans are used in their dried form, in Italy we most look forward to them when they are fresh and tiny, about as broad as a thumb tack, and so sweet and tender we eat them raw. When they are further into their season and have become medium sized, we cook them in several delicious ways.

Broad beans show up in Italian markets in time for an early Easter. Before the end of May they are already on their way out. Depending on the variety, young broad beans come about 4 to 5 in a pod not longer than 15cm/5 or 6in. Often they are still attached to a portion of their stem. At the end of the meal in southern *trattorie*, they will often bring out a basket full of *fave* still in their pods. As the shelling progresses table conversation becomes more animated, thanks to all the chilled white wine provided for washing down the beans. Often a huge hunk of local cheese will be added to the table, a perfect end to a warm, spring meal.

For a more formal luncheon, I combine the same ingredients as above, but shell the beans and dice the cheese and dress them with extra-virgin olive oil and cracked pepper. I use this as a *bruschetta* topping – slices of grilled country bread rubbed with garlic – and serve it as an antipasto or even a first course for a light meal.

Young bright green *fave* add wonderful colour to pasta or combined with shellfish or mixed with other spring vegetables, such as peas and asparagus. When they are more mature the thin outer skin of the *fave* takes on a pronounced bitter taste and the beans are better cooked, usually with a bit of *pancetta* or *prosciutto*.

BROAD BEANS
WITH PROSCIUTTO
Fave con il prosciutto

3 TBSP EXTRA-VIRGIN OLIVE OIL
90G/3OZ PROSCIUTTO, CHOPPED
1 WHITE ONION, CHOPPED
2KG/4½LB BROAD BEANS, PODDED BUT
UNPEELED
120ML/4FL OZ/½ CUP LIGHT CHICKEN
STOCK
1 ROUND LETTUCE
SALT AND PEPPER

Heat the oil in a large saucepan and fry the prosciutto with the onion over a low heat for about 3 minutes, until the onion is translucent. Add the beans, chicken stock and salt and pepper to taste, cover and cook for about 10 minutes. Meanwhile, cut the lettuce into julienne strips. Add to the beans and cook for a couple minutes more, stirring gently. Pour on to a platter and serve immediately.

Serves 6

BROAD BEANS
WITH CHEESE CREAM
Fave alla crema di formaggio

2KG/4½LB BROAD BEANS, SHELLED
300ML/10FL OZ/1¼ CUPS DOUBLE
(HEAVY) CREAM
90G/3OZ/½ CUP GRATED FONTINA
CHEESE
SALT AND PEPPER

Blanch the beans for 1 minute in a saucepan of boiling, salted water. Drain and rinse under cold water to keep them green. Pour back into the saucepan and add the cream. Cook, covered, over a low heat for about 10 minutes until tender. Add half the cheese and pepper to taste and mix gently. Arrange the beans on a platter, sprinkle with the remaining cheese and serve.

Serves 6

BROAD BEANS WITH FENNEL

FAVE AL FINOCCHIO

1 FENNEL BULB, SLICED PAPER THIN, GREEN FEATHERY
LEAVES RESERVED

3 TBSP EXTRA-VIRGIN OLIVE OIL

2KG/4½LB BROAD BEANS, SHELLED

120ML/4FLOZ/½ CUP LIGHT CHICKEN STOCK

FEW CHERRY TOMATOES

SALT AND PEPPER

Chop the feathery fennel leaves and reserve. Heat the oil in a saucepan, add the beans, fennel slices and stock and cook, covered, over a low heat for about 10 minutes, or until tender. Add the tomatoes and cook for 2 minutes more, to heat through. Add salt and pepper to taste. Arrange on a platter, sprinkle on the reserved fennel leaves and serve.

Serves 6

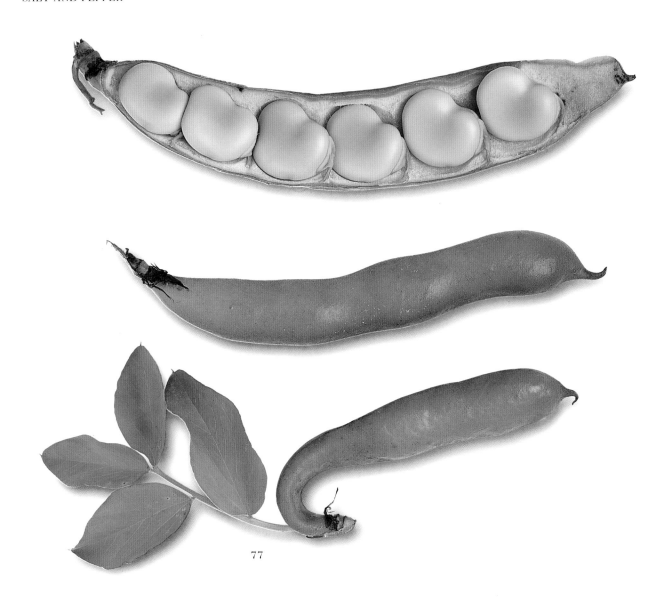

77

BORLOTTI BEANS

"*Full o'beans and benevolence*"

(ROBERT SMITH SURTEES 1805–1864, *HANDLEY CROSS*, 1854)

AN OLD ITALIAN ADAGE, based on the folk wisdom that you are what you eat, characterizes the inhabitants of the country according to their principal regional dish. Tuscans are *mangiafagioli*, bean-eaters, which implies they are "full of beans" in the metaphoric sense as well. Historically Tuscany was a poor, rural region and protein-rich beans were traditionally the "meat of the poor". As a result, now prosperous Tuscany has a vast repertoire of recipes using dozens of varieties of beans, especially dried.

The most colourful beans in the bag are the borlotti. They belong to the category referred to in English as cranberry beans, because both their pods and the beans themselves have cranberry-coloured markings, red speckles on pale rose.

Borlotti beans cook to a creamy consistency, which makes them best for purées and stews. They are used mostly in northern Italian cooking, from the regions of Veneto and Lombardia, where they are often paired with *polenta*.

Tuscans favour white beans, like the medium-sized cannellini, or their own local variety called *toscanelli*. A Tuscan white bean that was on the verge of extinction but is now enjoying a revival is the smaller and thinner skinned *zolfini*. These are the beans used for the Tuscan dish called *fagioli all'uccelletto*, "beans cooked like a little bird", that is, simmered in olive oil with garlic, sage and a little tomato pulp, the same way small game birds are braised in Tuscany. This dish is often served along with grilled pork sausages or roast pork. White beans also constitute the base of Tuscan *minestrone*, vegetable soup, which becomes *ribollita*, meaning "boiled again", when old bread is added to thicken leftover *minestrone* and reheated the next day.

Most cookery books will tell you to soak dried beans overnight before cooking. Instead, boil them for a couple of minutes and let them sit in their hot water for a while. Many bean varieties that are usually found in dried form are also eaten fresh in season. I cook these until soft, ladled over a slice of grilled country bread rubbed with garlic, dressed with the finest extra-virgin olive oil and topped with freshly ground black pepper. This makes a simple, delicious and nourishing light lunch by itself.

Another tasty way to use fresh beans, or dried ones for that matter, is in a salad combined with some chopped onion and the highest quality tuna preserved in olive oil.

BORLOTTI WITH CUTTLEFISH
Borlotti con le seppie

300G/10OZ DRIED BORLOTTI BEANS
3 TBSP EXTRA-VIRGIN OLIVE OIL
1 ONION, CHOPPED
3 GARLIC CLOVES, CHOPPED
300G/10OZ BABY CUTTLEFISH,
CLEANED AND SLICED IN HALF
LENGTHWISE
3 PLUM TOMATOES, PEELED, NOT
SEEDED, AND CHOPPED
1 TBSP CHOPPED FLAT-LEAF
ITALIAN PARSLEY
SALT AND PEPPER

Soak the beans in water overnight. Drain, place the beans in a saucepan and cover with fresh water. Bring to a slow boil and cook for about 1½ hours. Drain and reserve. Heat the oil in a saucepan and fry the onion and garlic over a low heat for about 3 minutes, until translucent. Add the cuttlefish to the pan. Sauté over a high heat for about 3 minutes, stirring, then add the tomatoes and the beans and lower the heat to medium. Cook for about 5 minutes, or until the liquid has evaporated. Add salt and pepper to taste, sprinkle with the parsley, mix gently and arrange on a platter. Serve immediately.

Serves 6

BORLOTTI SALAD
BORLOTTI IN INSALATA

300G/10OZ DRIED BORLOTTI BEANS
300G/10OZ CANNED TUNA IN OIL,
DRAINED
1 TBSP LEMON JUICE
1 RED ONION, PEELED AND
SLICED PAPER THIN
6 TBSP EXTRA-VIRGIN OLIVE OIL
SALT AND PEPPER

Soak the beans in water for about 12 hours. Drain, place the beans in a saucepan and cover with fresh water. Bring to a slow boil and cook for about 1½ hours. Drain and arrange in a bowl. Crumble the tuna and sprinkle with the lemon juice. Add the onion to the beans with the tuna, olive oil and salt and pepper to taste and mix gently. Serve at room temperature.

    Serves 6

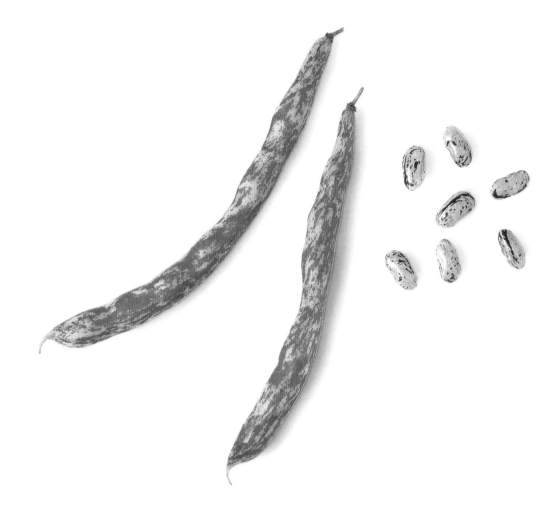

BORLOTTI AND RICE MINESTRONE
MINESTRONE DI RISO E BORLOTTI

210G/7OZ DRIED BORLOTTI BEANS
6 TBSP EXTRA-VIRGIN OLIVE OIL
1 CARROT, CHOPPED
1 ONION, CHOPPED
1 CELERY STALK, CHOPPED
1 TBSP CHOPPED FLAT-LEAF
ITALIAN PARSLEY
6 HANDFULS ARBORIO OR OTHER RICE
1.75 LITRE/3 PINT/6 CUPS VEGETABLE
STOCK
SALT AND PEPPER

Soak the beans in water for about 12 hours. Drain, place the beans in a saucepan and cover with fresh water. Bring to a slow boil and cook for about 1½ hours.

    Drain and reserve the water. Heat the oil in a saucepan and fry the carrot, onion, celery and parsley for about 3 minutes, stirring occasionally. Add the rice and mix well. Add the beans and vegetable stock and cook for 12 minutes. Add 2 ladles of the reserved water and salt and pepper to taste. Boil for 2 minutes more and then serve immediately.

    Serves 6

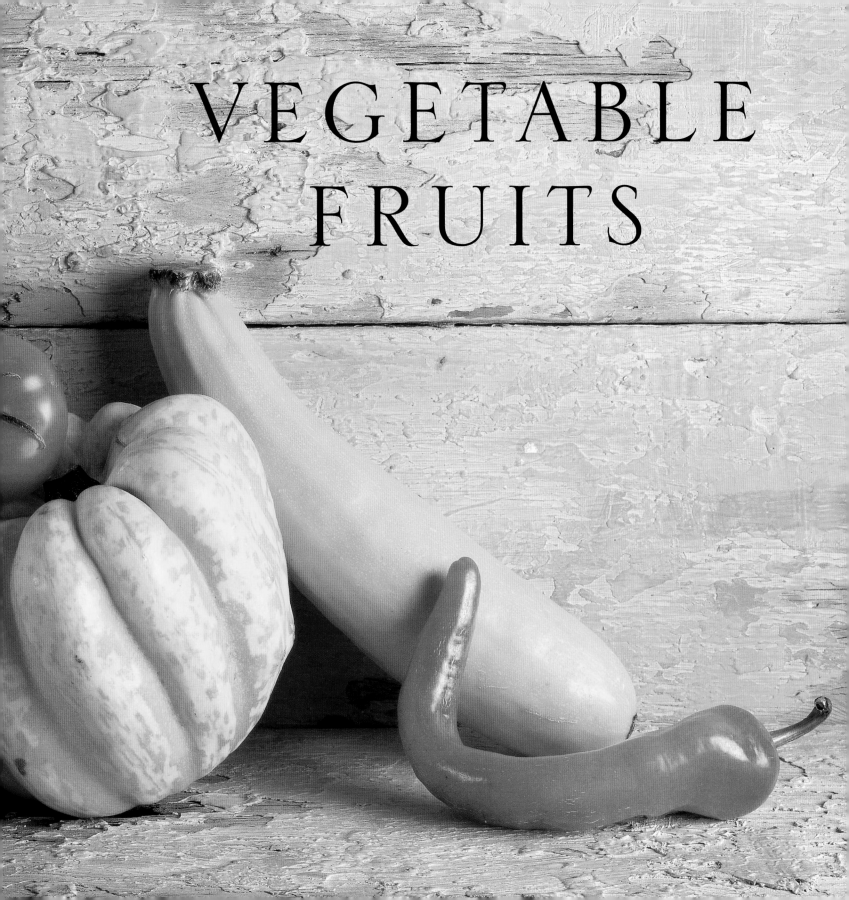

VEGETABLE FRUITS

AVOCADOS

(PERSEA AMERICANA)

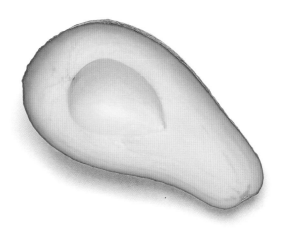

I TASTED MY FIRST AVOCADO when I was a young girl on holiday in England. I was more impressed by its looks than its flavour. Some years afterwards in the United States I was introduced to Mexican food and my first dish of guacamole, mashed avocado with chopped tomatoes and onions served with tortilla chips. That was delicious. I did not see avocados in Italy until much later and then only occasionally in the grander food shops of Milan. They were a curiosity, along with other exotic and tropical fruits.

Only relatively recently have avocados shown up in Italian markets, imported from Israel in the winter and South Africa in the summer. One of my sons had a girlfriend from southern California, whose hometown called itself the "avocado capital of the world". She brought us some from her family's ranch and these were the best I have ever tasted, with a rich, nutty flavour and buttery texture.

I know of no recipes for cooking avocados, although they probably exist. We use them fresh, usually in salads. They combine particularly well with citrus fruit, oranges or grapefruit and a squeeze of lemon or lime, which balances their high oil content. Most simply, I slice an avocado in half, remove the seed and fill the cavity with extra-virgin olive oil and a little ground black pepper. The English like them with shellfish (my first avocado was served with prawns) and I have found they go well with smoked fish. One of the tastiest ways to use the avocado is in any variation of classic guacamole. I purée the traditional ingredients, avocado, tomatoes and onion, in a blender and serve them as a sauce for boiled rice or grilled vegetables.

AVOCADO AND ORANGE SALAD
Avocado in insalata con arance

3 AVOCADOS
2 ORANGES, PEELED AND SLICED
1 WHITE ONION, THINLY SLICED
1 TBSP LEMON JUICE
4 TBSP EXTRA-VIRGIN OLIVE OIL
SALT AND PEPPER

Peel the avocados and discard the stone. Slice them thinly and arrange on a platter. Arrange the orange slices around the avocado. Sprinkle the onion over the fruits. Dissolve a little salt with the lemon juice, mix with the oil and pour over everything. Sprinkle with pepper and serve.

Serves 6

86

AVOCADO WITH SMOKED HERRING

AVOCADO ALLE ARINGHE AFFUMICATE

3 AVOCADOS
JUICE OF 1 LEMON
1 FILLET OF SMOKED HERRING, CHOPPED
1 SMALL ONION, SLICED PAPER THIN INTO RINGS
3 TBSP EXTRA-VIRGIN OLIVE OIL
PEPPER

Slice the avocados in half horizontally and discard the stones. Sprinkle the flesh with the lemon juice. Put a little herring fillet in each avocado cavity and sprinkle the onion rings over the herring. Pour a little olive oil over each avocado, sprinkle with pepper and serve.

Serves 6

AVOCADO SAUCE

SALSA DI AVOCADO

1 AVOCADO
1 RIPE TOMATO
1 SPRING ONION (SCALLION), THINLY SLICED
1 TBSP LEMON JUICE
1 TSP GRATED LEMON ZEST
3 TBSP EXTRA-VIRGIN OLIVE OIL
SALT AND PEPPER

Peel, stone and dice the avocado. Blanch the tomato for 30 seconds in boiling water then peel. Put the avocado, tomato and onion into a blender. Add the lemon juice and zest, the oil and salt and pepper to taste and purée until creamy. Add the sauce to grilled vegetables or pour over cold, boiled rice.

Serves 6

TOMATOES

(LYCOPERSICON)

THE TASTE OF a perfectly ripe tomato straight off the vine and still warm from the sun I rate as a peak gastronomic experience. Food historians tell us the tomato originated in South America and arrived in the Old World, probably first in Italy, most likely brought back by Columbus from one of his voyages to the Americas. In any case, Italian cooking, especially southern Italian cooking, has not been the same since. The tomato lends its goodness to countless sauces and numerous dishes. For the first couple of hundred years after its arrival in Europe, the tomato was considered an exotic plant and its culinary use was rare. The first written recipe using tomatoes is found in a seventeenth-century cookery book from Naples for a tomato sauce flavoured with garlic, onion and parsley. Only in the early nineteenth century, again in Naples, did the cultivation and canning of tomatoes develop on an industrial scale.

Dozens of varieties of tomato are now grown in Italy. The first to arrive at market is the type that looks like a large cherry and comes in a cluster still attached to the vine. These cherry tomatoes, *pomodorini* or *ciliegini*, literally burst with sweetness and flavour. All you need do is slice them in half and dress them with extra-virgin olive oil and a few fresh basil leaves. If they are bite-sized, you can leave them whole and pop them into your mouth like cherries. The best tomato for cooking is the San Marzano, a so-called plum variety, because of its thin, elongated shape. Its intense flavour and firm flesh with less seeds and juice than other types make it ideal for sauces and preserving. Around midsummer I look forward to the large and ribbed beefsteak tomatoes from my garden. I pick them when they are still greenish-orange and stuff them with rice or seafood.

You can best judge and appreciate a good tomato when you remember that botanically it is a fruit. Only because of its uses in cooking has it come to be thought of as a vegetable. Accordingly, when shopping for tomatoes you should look for the same qualities you would want to find, say, in a perfect peach. Most importantly tomatoes must be in season. During winter and early spring use high-quality tomato preserves and take pleasure in looking forward to the arrival of fresh tomatoes in summer.

FRESH TOMATO SAUCE
SALSA AL POMODORO FRESCO

1KG/2¼LB VERY RIPE PLUM TOMATOES
6 GARLIC CLOVES
120ML/4FL OZ/½ CUP EXTRA-VIRGIN
OLIVE OIL
1 CHILLI PEPPER
1 HANDFUL ROCKET (ARUGULA)
LEAVES
SALT

Bring a large saucepan of water to the boil, add the tomatoes and cook for 30 seconds. Drain and peel.

Peel the garlic and mash with a fork. Heat half the oil in a saucepan and sauté the garlic and chilli over a low heat for about 3 minutes, or until barely golden. Add the tomatoes and a little salt and cook over a high heat for 3 minutes more, stirring gently, to keep the tomatoes whole. Add the rocket (arugula), mix well then pour into a dish and serve.

Serves 6

BAKED TOMATOES
POMODORI IN TORTIERA

12 MEDIUM RIPE SALAD TOMATOES,
WASHED AND DRIED
2 TBSP CASTER (SUPERFINE) SUGAR
3 TBSP BALSAMIC VINEGAR
SALT

Preheat the oven to 170°C/350°F/gas mark 3.

Halve the tomatoes and sprinkle the cut parts with a little salt. Sprinkle the sugar into the bottom of an ovenproof dish and arrange the tomatoes in one layer, cut side down. Pour the balsamic vinegar over them and cook in the oven for about 1 hour, or until the liquid has evaporated and the tomatoes are almost caramelized. Serve hot.

Serves 6

BAKED PLUM TOMATOES
POMODORI IN TEGLIA

3 TBSP CASTER (SUPERFINE) SUGAR
3 TBSP EXTRA-VIRGIN OLIVE OIL
18 RIPE PLUM TOMATOES, WASHED,
DRIED AND CUT IN HALF
SALT

Preheat the oven to 130°C/250°F/gas mark ½.

Mix the sugar and oil, add salt to taste and spread the mixture in the bottom of an ovenproof dish. Arrange the tomatoes on top, cut-side down, in one layer. Bake in the oven for 1 hour, until the liquid has evaporated. Serve around fish or meat, or on pasta or rice.

Serves 6

TOMATOES FILLED WITH MOZZARELLA
POMODORI RIPIENI DI MOZZARELLA

18 RIPE PLUM TOMATOES, WASHED AND DRIED
300G/10OZ MOZZARELLA CHEESE, DICED
6 TBSP EXTRA-VIRGIN OLIVE OIL
3 TBSP CAPERS IN SALT, WELL WASHED
18 BASIL LEAVES
SALT AND PEPPER

Preheat the oven to 180°C/375°F/gas mark 4.

Cut the tomatoes in half horizontally, scoop out the flesh and discard. Mix the mozzarella with the oil and capers. Fill one half of each tomato with the mozzarella and caper mixture and add salt and pepper to taste. Cover with the basil leaves and top each with the reserved halves. Bake in the oven for about 40 minutes, then arrange on a platter and serve.

Serves 6

CUCUMBERS

(CUCUMIS SATIVUS)

"*A cucumber should be well sliced, and dressed with pepper and vinegar, and then thrown out as good for nothing.*"

(SAMUEL JOHNSON, QUOTED IN BOSWELL'S *JOURNAL OF A TOUR TO THE HEBRIDES WITH SAMUEL JOHNSON*, OCT. 5, 1773)

ALTHOUGH CUCUMBERS are available in any Italian market all twelve months of the year, it never occurs to me to buy them until I feel the first heat of the summer (their natural season, by the way). Then I actually long for their cooling, refreshing flavour. The cucumber, *cetriolo* in Italian, is one of the principal ingredients of the traditional Tuscan summer salad, *panzanella*, made of dried bread and raw vegetables, in particular tomatoes and onions, and dressed with extra-virgin olive oil and red wine vinegar. Sliced, juicy cucumbers add a crisp, crunchy texture to the composition.

Cucumbers are one of the few vegetables that Columbus introduced to the New World from the Old, instead of the other way round. They were first cultivated in the Orient thousands of years before arriving in Europe and belong to the same family of vine-like plants as watermelon and other melons. Of the several varieties of cucumbers, the small ones with green, spiny skin, called gherkins, are used for pickling, whereas the large fruit is eaten fresh. The so-called Mediterranean-type has a smooth, dark green skin and can grow very long, although it is usually harvested when it is about 12.5–20.5cm/5–8in in length. When very fresh its skin is tender enough to be eaten along with its flesh and its mild flavour is similar to a melon.

I am still waiting for some young, imaginative chef to come up with a few new and interesting ways to cook cucumbers. I sauté them for a few minutes, add yogurt and season with chilli powder, chives and poppy seeds. Chilled, this makes a delicious dip. I have included a recipe for sweet and sour cucumbers which I serve as a side dish.

GINGERED CUCUMBER SALAD
CETRIOLI ALLO ZENZERO

6 CUCUMBERS, PEELED

1 CARROT, PEELED

1 TBSP RED WINE VINEGAR

4 TBSP EXTRA-VIRGIN OLIVE OIL

1 SMALL PIECE OF GINGER, PEELED

GRATED ZEST OF 1 LEMON

SALT

Slice the cucumbers crosswise. Cut the carrot into julienne strips. Mix the cucumber and carrot in a salad bowl. Dissolve a little salt to taste with the vinegar, add the oil and mix well then pour over the vegetables. Toss the salad, grate some ginger on top, add the lemon zest and serve.

Serves 6

94

CUCUMBERS WITH CHIVES

CETRIOLI ALL'ERBA CIPOLLINA

3 TBSP EXTRA-VIRGIN OLIVE OIL

6 CUCUMBERS, PEELED, DESEEDED
AND DICED

1 PINCH CHILLI POWDER

60ML/2FL OZ/⅓ CUP YOGURT

1 TBSP POPPY SEEDS

1 TBSP CHOPPED CHIVES

SALT

Heat the oil in a saucepan over a low heat, add the cucumbers and sprinkle with the chilli and salt to taste. Cover and cook, shaking occasionally, for about 10 minutes. Add the yogurt and cook until heated through. Pour on to a serving dish, sprinkle with the poppy seeds and chives and serve.

Serves 6

SWEET AND SOUR CUCUMBERS

CETRIOLI IN AGRODOLCE

6 CUCUMBERS, PEELED, DESEEDED AND DICED

1 LARGE WHITE ONION, CHOPPED

1 GARLIC CLOVE, CHOPPED

3 TBSP EXTRA-VIRGIN OLIVE OIL

3 TBSP WHITE WINE VINEGAR

1 TBSP GRANULATED SUGAR

SALT AND PEPPER

Bring a little water in a saucepan to the boil, add the cucumbers and cook for a few minutes, until translucent. Drain and arrange in a bowl, adding salt to taste. Fry the onion and garlic in the oil over a low heat for about 5 minutes, or until barely golden. Add the vinegar, sugar and a little salt and pepper to taste. Fry for a couple of minutes more then pour over the cucumber. Leave it to rest for a couple of hours before serving at room temperature.

Serves 6

MUSHROOMS

(MUSSIRIO)

"I am ... a mushroom
On whom the dew of heaven drops now and then."

WHERE I LIVE IN TUSCANY, when we say mushroom we think *porcini*, the *Boletus edulis*. *Porcini* means "little pigs", which describes this mushroom's fat, squat shape and dirty brown colour. Besides several varieties of the *Boletus*, dozens of other edible wild mushrooms thrive in the thick Tuscan woods. My favourite by far is the delicious *ovolo* or *Amanita caesarea*, *Caesaris* mushroom, truly fit for a king.

When they are young, *ovoli* are completely enclosed in an egg-shaped and egg-coloured volva that opens later to reveal a beautiful yolk-orange cap. They make a superb salad, thinly sliced, mixed with paper thin shavings of Parmesan and dressed with a little lemon juice and extra-virgin olive oil. Add thin strips of white celery for a contrast in texture.

Porcini have two seasons in Tuscany, usually a brief one in late spring and an extended one in autumn, both periods of the year when the climatic combination of rain and heat produces the humidity that causes them to pop up from the warm and damp woodland soil. I never let a season pass without enjoying the luxury of eating a meaty *porcini* cap on its own. It is equal, if not better, than the finest filet mignons and, depending on the season, can be just about as expensive. There are several ways to prepare and cook the cap. The easiest is to drizzle it with extra-virgin olive oil, salt and pepper, add fresh mint, wrap in aluminum foil and bake for about 15 minutes. You can also grill them over an open fire. This method seems to bring out their earthy flavour and aroma. My family likes to stick slivers of garlic into the cap before grilling. A little more complicated but absolutely delicious way to celebrate the cap is to arrange them on skewers, alternating with *pancetta* and bay leaves and cook under a grill. Before serving, dress with a sauce of parsley and extra-virgin olive oil.

A tasty recipe for *porcini* that I learned from my youngest son is to deep-fry them. This is a good way to use fresh *porcini* that are not in perfect shape, which is often the case with wild mushrooms. All he does is dust the whole mushroom with a little flour, dip in a simple egg batter, coat with dry breadcrumbs and fry. Eat them while they are still hot as an aperitif with a glass of good Chianti Classico wine.

When preparing wild mushrooms for cooking, it is important to clean them with as little water as possible. I usually wipe them with a damp cloth and pare off any stubborn soil at the end of the stem.

MUSHROOM CAPS WITH BAY LEAVES
TESTE DI FUNGHI ALL'ALLORO

30 MUSHROOM CAPS (PORCINI OR
CHAMPIGNONS)
6 SLICES OF PANCETTA OR BACON
24 BAY LEAVES
4 TBSP EXTRA-VIRGIN OLIVE OIL
1 TBSP LEMON JUICE
2 TBSP FINELY CHOPPED FLAT-LEAF
ITALIAN PARSLEY
SALT AND PEPPER

Preheat the grill to warm.

Clean the mushrooms with a damp cloth, but do not wash them. Cut the pancetta or bacon into 24 pieces. Alternate on 6 skewers the mushroom caps with the pancetta and the bay leaves. Brush with a little of the oil. Cook under the grill, turning the skewers often, for about 10 minutes.

Mix the remaining oil with the lemon juice and the parsley. Arrange the skewers on a platter, pour the parsley-oil mixture over them and serve.

Serves 6

DEEP-FRIED MUSHROOMS
FUNGHI FRITTI

600G/1¼LB PORCINI OR SHIITAKE
MUSHROOMS
90G/3OZ/½ CUP PLAIN
(ALL-PURPOSE) FLOUR
2 EGGS
300G/10OZ FINE DRIED BREADCRUMBS
1 LITRE/1¾ PINT/4 CUPS OIL
SALT AND PEPPER

Clean the mushrooms with a damp cloth, but do not wash them. Cut them into 1cm/⅜in slices and put them in a paper bag with the flour. Shake the bag to coat the mushrooms in flour. Beat the eggs in a deep dish. Dip each mushroom in the egg wash and then in the breadcrumbs to coat well. Heat the oil in a frying pan to 170°C/350°F. Fry the mushrooms, a few at a time, for about 5 minutes, or until barely golden. Drain them on a paper towel, arrange on a platter and serve immediately, very hot.

Serves 6

MUSHROOM SALAD
INSALATA DI FUNGHI

300G/10OZ PORCINI OR, PREFERABLY, OVOLI MUSHROOMS
(AMANITA PURPUREA)
90G/3OZ PIECE PARMESAN CHEESE
2 WHITE CELERY STALKS, CUT INTO JULIENNE STRIPS
1 TSP LEMON JUICE
4 TBSP EXTRA-VIRGIN OLIVE OIL
SALT AND PEPPER

Clean the mushrooms with a damp cloth and slice finely with a mandoline. With the mandoline, slice the Parmesan paper thin. Arrange the mushrooms in a salad bowl, cover with the celery and the Parmesan. Sprinkle with salt and pepper, lemon juice and the oil and serve.

Serves 6

PEPPERS & CHILLIS

(CAPSICUM FRUTESCENS)

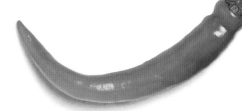

"*P*eter Piper picked a peck of pickled pepper"

(Nursery Rhyme)

*C*APSICUM IS THE BOTANICAL NAME for the genus of plants that includes, among many other species, sweet and hot peppers. Sweet peppers are sometimes called bell peppers, because of their shape, really more like a barrel than a bell, or green peppers because of their colour, which can also be yellow, orange and red.

Sweet peppers in Italian are called *peperoni*, "big peppers".

In Italy hot peppers are called *peperoncini*, little peppers and one tiny, bright red variety is named *diavolillo*, "little devil", hotter than hell. In English hot peppers are called chillis or chili peppers. I always assumed they got that name from the eponymous island but it turns out it is really a corruption of a Central America Indian word. Capsicums were brought back from the Americas to Europe by Columbus.

As I child I consumed my fair share of sweet peppers along with other raw vegetables, when we were served *bagna cauda* at my grandmother's castle near Asti in Piedmont, a region renowned for its handsome and meaty sweet peppers. The most traditional Southern Italian recipe for sweet peppers is called *peperonata*, stewed in tomato sauce with onions and garlic. It is served as a side dish with the meat course. Sweet

peppers were made for stuffing, a perfect, practically hollow shape. Rice is the classic filling, while in the southern regions they sometimes stuff them with dressed pasta. Happily, sweet peppers have been favoured by the new generation of restaurant cooks. Now, colourful and tasty roasted peppers appear on many fine menus. Grilled and sautéed they make an especially delicious pasta sauce. A popular dish served at our Coltibuono winery restaurant is a mellow yellow and red pepper soup.

Chillis are used in Italian cooking more for their flavour than the sensation of heat, which is so prized by palates in Latin America. A family favourite of ours, especially when my children were young and always hungry and also in my youth when we needed a quick midnight pickup, is a bowl of spaghetti dressed with the sauce called *aglio, olio e peperoncino*, simply lots of garlic sautéed in extra-virgin olive oil with an addition of dried chillis to taste. Tuscany's most famous butcher, Dario Cecchini, makes a kind of preserve with chillis and sugar that he calls *mostarda mediterranea*. It is a flavourful combination of sweet and hot that makes your tongue tingle and goes wonderfully with cheese or meat, pork in particular.

STEWED PEPPERS WITH RICE MOULDS
Peperonata con sformatini di riso

6 RED AND YELLOW PEPPERS
480G/1LB/2 CUPS RICE (ANY QUALITY)
120ML/4FL OZ/½ CUP EXTRA-VIRGIN OLIVE OIL
3 GARLIC CLOVES
1 HANDFUL FRESH BASIL LEAVES
SALT AND PEPPER

Preheat the oven to 200°C/400°F/gas mark 6.

Put the peppers in a baking dish and cook in the oven for about 30 minutes until soft. Place in a bag for about 10 minutes to soften the skins. Halve and peel the peppers, discard the seeds and slice them. Sprinkle with salt and keep them warm. Bring a large saucepan of water to the boil, add a little salt and the rice. Cook until *al dente* – about 10 minutes for basmati, 14 minutes for arborio, then drain and keep warm. Meanwhile, in a blender, cream the oil, garlic and basil with a little salt and pepper. Mix well with the rice and press into 6 individual moulds or ramekins. Immediately turn each one out on to a dish, surround with the peppers and serve.

Serves 6

PEPPERS WITH ANCHOVY SAUCE
Peperoni alle acciughe

6 RED OR YELLOW PEPPERS
3 GARLIC CLOVES, CHOPPED
3 ANCHOVY FILLETS IN OIL, DRAINED
5 TBSP EXTRA-VIRGIN OLIVE OIL
3 TBSP DRIED FINE BREADCRUMBS
SALT

Preheat the oven to 170°C/350°F/gas mark 3.

Put the peppers in a baking dish and cook in the oven for about 40 minutes. Place them in a bag for about 10 minutes to soften the skins. Peel them, cut in half and discard the seeds. Slice the peppers, arrange on a platter and add salt to taste. Fry the garlic and the anchovies in the oil for 1 minute, add the breadcrumbs and sauté, stirring continuously, for about 3 minutes, or until the breadcrumbs are barely golden. Sprinkle the sauce on to the peppers and serve.

Serves 6

CHILLI OIL
OLIO AL PEPERONCINO

480ML/16FL OZ/2 CUPS EXTRA-VIRGIN
OLIVE OIL
6 GARLIC CLOVES
90G/3OZ SMALL RED CHILLIES

Pour the oil into a clean bottle, add the garlic and the chillies. Let stand in a dark place for about 2 weeks. Drain the oil into a bowl and discard the garlic cloves. Pour the oil and chillies back into the bottle. This oil can be stored for up to 3 years. Use in sauces, pasta dishes or with rice.

Makes about 480ml/16fl oz/2 cups of chilli oil

AUBERGINE

(SOLANUM MELONGENA)

THE NEW WORLD NAME for this vegetable fruit is more descriptive than the French aubergine or the Italian *melanzane.* In North America and Australia it is called eggplant and eggfruit, respectively. Although the most common type of aubergine is oval-shaped and purple, there are varieties that are white and shaped like the egg of some large bird. The Italian name is interesting. Literally it means "apple of madness". In medieval times, when the aubergine arrived in Italy from India, new and exotic fruits were often called apples of some sort. People were suspicious of the strange and glossy fruit of the unusual aubergine plant and feared it was unhealthy. For several centuries, in fact, aubergines were grown as an ornamental plant, admired for their handsome green-grey leaves and tiny purple flowers. It was only in Renaissance times that this prejudice was overcome and *melanzane* made it to the table.

Aubergines thrive in warm weather climates. In Italy, especially in the south, several varieties are grown. The most common is called "Black Beauty", deep purple and oval-shaped with a little green cap. Vendors in Naples are proud of their *violetta lunga di Napoli*, slender, elongated and unmistakably phallic. Tuscany's *violetta di Firenze* is light purple and globe-shaped with a violet cap.

One reason why aubergines are so popular is that they combine beautifully with all the characteristic Mediterranean flavours – garlic, capers, peppers, tomatoes, basil and cheese, especially mozzarella and Parmesan. In Italy we fry, grill, bake and stuff them. In the south they even layer slices of aubergine spread with chocolate sauce and serve it as a dessert. At first glance and taste you might think you were eating a kind of *mille-feuille* pastry.

Be sure to buy aubergines that are fresh and light in weight, with shiny and firm skin. They will be tender and sweet and will not require that you go through the process of salting and draining them to draw out excessive water. Over-ripe aubergines develop bitter seeds and tough skin. As raw aubergines absorb olive oil like a sponge, it is better to add a little oil after they are cooked.

AUBERGINE WITH MOZZARELLA AND TOMATOES
MELANZANE ALLA NAPOLETANA

6 LONG AUBERGINES (EGGPLANT)
6 RIPE PLUM TOMATOES
1 HANDFUL FRESH BASIL LEAVES
4 TBSP EXTRA-VIRGIN OLIVE OIL
180G/6OZ MOZZARELLA CHEESE, DICED
SALT AND PEPPER

Preheat the oven to 170°C/350°F/gas mark 3.

Slice away the top of the aubergines (eggplant) horizontally and discard part of the pulp. Blanch the tomatoes in boiling water for 1 minute, then peel and dice them. Tear the basil leaves with your fingers. Mix the tomatoes with 3 tablespoons of the oil, a little salt and pepper and the basil. Fill the aubergines with the mozzarella, cover with the tomatoes and arrange them on a baking tray (cookie sheet) brushed with the remaining oil. Cook them in the oven for about 40 minutes, then arrange on a platter and serve.

Serves 6

AUBERGINE RICE
RISO ALLE MELANZANE

6 TBSP EXTRA-VIRGIN OLIVE OIL
3 GARLIC CLOVES, CHOPPED
2 AUBERGINES (EGGPLANT), DICED
3 VERY RIPE PLUM TOMATOES, PEELED
AND DICED
12 HANDFULS LONG GRAIN RICE
2 TBSP DRIED OREGANO
SALT AND PEPPER

Heat half the oil in a pan and sauté the garlic for about 3 minutes, or until translucent. Add the aubergine (eggplant) and sauté for about 5 minutes over a low heat, stirring occasionally. Add the tomatoes and salt and pepper to taste, cover and cook for about 20 minutes, or until the liquid has evaporated. Meanwhile, bring a large saucepan of water to the boil, add a little salt and the rice. Cook for about 12 minutes, until al dente, then drain and mix with the remaining oil. Pile the rice on a platter, pour the aubergines on top, sprinkle with the oregano and serve immediately.

Serves 6

GRILLED AUBERGINES WITH BASIL SAUCE

MELANZANE ALLA GRIGLIA CON SALSA DI BASILICO

4 TBSP EXTRA-VIRGIN OLIVE OIL
2 HANDFULS FRESH BASIL LEAVES,
CHOPPED
2 GARLIC CLOVES, FINELY CHOPPED
1 TBSP CAPERS IN VINEGAR, DRAINED
AND CHOPPED
6 LONG AUBERGINES (EGGPLANT)
SALT AND PEPPER

Preheat the grill to medium.

Reserve 2 tablespoons of the oil and mix the basil with the remainder. Add the garlic, capers and salt and pepper to taste and mix well. Cut the aubergines (eggplant) lengthwise into slices about 4mm/⅛in thick and brush them with the reserved oil. Cook under the grill for 2 minutes on each side, turning them carefully. The grill should not be too hot otherwise the aubergines will burn. Arrange them on a platter, sprinkle with the basil sauce and serve immediately.

Serves 6

PUMPKINS & SQUASH

(CUCURBITA)

"We fancy men are individuals; so are pumpkins;
but every pumpkin in the field goes through every point
of pumpkin history."

(R.W. EMERSON 1803–1882, "NOMINALIST AND REALIST," *ESSAYS: SECOND SERIES*, 1844)

MY FIRST MEMORY of pumpkins is not of Halloween, a celebration unknown in Italy when I was a child, but of autumnal family drives in the countryside outside Milan. We would stop at roadside stalls for a snack of baked pumpkin slices sprinkled with sugar. Those local pumpkins did not at all resemble the smooth-skinned Halloween variety. Our *zucca gialla* have a gnarled yellow-green exterior and inside their orange pulp is sweet and tasty.

A traditional way of preparing pumpkin in the regions of Lombardia and Veneto is to deep-fry slices in olive oil, pour boiling hot vinegar over the slices and marinate them for several hours before eating. In Mantova a classic pasta dish is *tortelli* stuffed with pumpkin seasoned with nutmeg and sugar and dressed with melted butter and cheese. The rich and spicy sweet taste of this dish is reminiscent of Renaissance cooking. Another classic regional dish is potato and pumpkin gnocchi. You purée baked potatoes and pumpkin, mix with a little flour, nutmeg and powdered bitter almond *amaretti* cookies and shape into gnocchi. When they are cooked, sprinkle them with freshly grated Parmesan, a little ground black pepper and dress with melted butter.

These sweet and savoury winter squash recipes predate American pumpkin pie by many centuries. Most contemporary palates probably prefer pumpkin as a dessert, so I have included my recipe for pumpkin cake, which uses much the same seasoning with eggs and sugar plus a squeeze of lemon juice.

SWEET AND SOUR PUMPKIN
Zucca in agrodolce

2KG/4½LB PUMPKIN, PEELED AND SEEDED
1 LITRE/1¾ PINT/4 CUPS OIL FOR DEEP-FRYING
60ML/2FL OZ/4 TBSP RED WINE VINEGAR
60G/2OZ/4 TBSP SUGAR
1 HANDFUL FRESH MINT LEAVES
SALT

Cut the pumpkin pulp into 1cm/⅜in slices. Heat the oil in a pan to 170°C/350°F, add the pumpkin slices a few at a time and deep-fry for about 5 minutes. Drain on absorbent paper. Boil the vinegar and the sugar in a small pan for a couple of minutes. Arrange the pumpkin slices in a large frying pan, pour the vinegar mixture over and cook until almost evaporated. Sprinkle with the mint and add salt to taste. Mix gently, arrange on a platter and serve.

Serves 6

PUMPKIN GNOCCHI
Gnocchi di zucca

480G/1LB BOILING POTATOES, WASHED
480G/1LB PUMPKIN, PEELED AND SEEDED
210G/7OZ/1⅘ CUPS PLAIN (ALL-PURPOSE) FLOUR
3 AMARETTO COOKIES, GROUND TO A POWDER
PINCH OF GRATED NUTMEG
2 EGG YOLKS
90G/3OZ/6 TBSP UNSALTED BUTTER
60G/2OZ/4 TBSP FRESHLY GRATED PARMESAN CHEESE
SALT AND PEPPER

Preheat the oven to 180°C/375°F/gas mark 4.

Wrap the potatoes in foil. Cut the pumpkin into pieces about the size of the potatoes and wrap them in foil, too. Cook the potatoes and pumpkin in the oven for about 1 hour, or until tender. Peel the potatoes. Purée the potatoes and the pumpkin through a ricer, then add half the flour, the amaretto powder, nutmeg, egg yolks and salt to taste. Use the remaining flour for your hands and to flour a baking tray (cookie sheet). Using floured hands, form little balls of purée about the size of a walnut, and place them on the floured tray. Bring a large saucepan of water to the boil. Add salt and lower in the gnocchi, a few at a time. When they come to the surface, drain them with a slotted spoon and arrange on a serving platter. Meanwhile, melt the butter over a low heat. When the gnocchi are cooked, sprinkle them with the Parmesan cheese, a little pepper and the butter and serve immediately while hot.

Serves 6

PUMPKIN CAKE
TORTA DI ZUCCA

3 LARGE EGGS, SEPARATED
180G/6OZ/1 CUP GRANULATED SUGAR
½ TBSP/1 ENVELOPE BAKING POWDER
240G/8OZ ALMONDS, FINELY CHOPPED
PINCH OF GRATED NUTMEG
GRATED ZEST OF 1 LEMON
6 TBSP PLAIN (ALL-PURPOSE) FLOUR
300G/10OZ PUMPKIN, CUT INTO
JULIENNE STRIPS
A LITTLE BUTTER FOR GREASING

Preheat the oven to 170°C/350°F/gas mark 3.

In a bowl, beat the egg yolks with the sugar until fluffy. Add the baking powder, almonds, nutmeg, lemon zest, 5 tablespoons of the flour and the pumpkin. Mix until well blended. Beat the egg whites and fold them gently into the batter. Butter a 23cm/9in springform tin and dust with the remaining flour. Pour the batter into the tin and cook in the oven for about 1 hour, covering the top with foil after 40 minutes of cooking. Cool on a wire rack, then turn out on to a platter and serve at room temperature.

Makes 1 x 23cm/9in cake

SWEET CORN

(ZEA MAYS SACCHARATA)

WHEN YOU DRIVE THROUGH the Italian countryside, in the north especially, you will come upon extensive fields of corn. Do not, however, look forward to eating corn-on-the-cob when you stop at a local restaurant. Most of the cultivation you see is destined to become animal feed or be processed into cornmeal. Sweet corn as a table food has never caught on in Italy. My children developed a taste for sweet corn during their stays in America. I tried growing it in my garden at Coltibuono, but our cool summer nights defeated my efforts.

Maize, *granturco*, of which sweet corn is a variety, arrived in Europe from America and became very popular in the Italian regions of the Veneto and Lombardia. It is ground into flour, *farina gialla*, "yellow flour" or cornmeal, and used for making polenta. The cornmeal is boiled and stirred constantly. When it has achieved the desired consistency, it is served hot, usually dressed with a savoury sauce. Polenta is also fried, grilled and baked.

Sweet corn, cultivated in the southern regions of Italy, has begun to appear in the vegetable markets of major Italian cities. Street vendors in the south grill corn-on-the-cob, protected in their husks, over a very hot fire. You eat it on the spot, sprinkled with salt. In restaurants sweet corn kernels are now frequently included in a mixed salad. I combine them with thinly sliced mushroom caps and cheese.

SWEET CORN SOUP
MINESTRA DI GRANTURCO

1KG/2¼LB SWEET CORN,
HUSKS REMOVED
3 TBSP EXTRA-VIRGIN OLIVE OIL
1 WHITE ONION, CHOPPED
120G/4OZ PANCETTA, CHOPPED
2 LITRE/3½ PINT/8 CUPS
VEGETABLE STOCK
2 TBSP CHOPPED FLAT-LEAF
ITALIAN PARSLEY
SALT AND PEPPER

Using a sharp knife, strip the kernels from the cobs. Heat the oil in a saucepan and cook the onion and pancetta, stirring constantly, for about 3 minutes, or until slightly golden and crisp. Add the corn, stock and salt and pepper to taste and bring to the boil. Simmer for about 1 hour, then pour into a soup tureen, add the parsley and serve hot.
Serves 6

SWEET CORN WITH FRESH TOMATO
Granturco al pomodoro

1KG/2¼LB SWEET CORN, HUSKS REMOVED
480G/1LB RIPE PLUM TOMATOES, PEELED BUT NOT SEEDED, AND CHOPPED
1 WHITE ONION, CHOPPED
60G/2OZ/4 TBSP UNSALTED BUTTER
2 TBSP CHOPPED CHIVES
SALT AND PEPPER

Steam the corn cobs over a saucepan of boiling water for about 10 minutes. Drain and cool slightly then strip the kernels from the cobs. Put the corn and the tomatoes in a saucepan. Add the onion and salt and pepper to taste, and cook over a low heat, stirring occasionally, until the cooking liquid has evaporated. Add the butter and sprinkle with the chives. Mix until the butter has melted then arrange on a platter and serve.

Serves 6

SWEET CORN AND MUSHROOM SALAD
Insalata di granturco e funghi

480G/1LB SWEET CORN, HUSKS REMOVED
210G/7OZ CULTIVATED MUSHROOMS
210G/7OZ FONTINA CHEESE OR SIMILAR, SLICED PAPER THIN
4 TBSP EXTRA-VIRGIN OLIVE OIL
SALT AND PEPPER

Bring a large saucepan of water to the boil, add a little salt and the corn cobs. Cook for about 10 minutes, drain and cool then strip the kernels from the cobs, and arrange them in a salad bowl. Separate the mushroom caps from the stems. Discard the stems or use for another dish. Wipe the caps clean and slice them thinly vertically. Add the mushrooms and cheese to the salad bowl and sprinkle with salt and pepper. Add the oil, mix gently and serve.

Serves 6

ZUCCHINI
(COURGETTE)

I WOULD LIKE TO make one thing clear from the start. Zucchini should be called zucchini, not courgettes, as some French chef in London must have done decades ago, with the result that the name has stuck ever since among many English-speaking peoples, especially recipe editors, much to my chagrin. In France their full name is *courgettes d'Italie*. I take the learned opinion of the English food historian Alan Davidson as definitive on this question. He writes in *The Oxford Companion to Food*, " . . .it seems clear that it was the Italians who first marketed [zucchini] and it is therefore appropriate to choose their name, zucchini, rather than the French name, courgettes, as the adopted English name."

Zucchini means "little squash", and the name describes their gastronomic nature. They are meant to be eaten small, 10–15cm/4–6in. If left on the vine too long, they will continue to grow, develop seeds and blemishes on their skin and their flesh will turn mushy and bitter. When harvested in time, late spring and early summer, they are shiny green, firm to the touch and have a subtly sweet and delicate flavour.

Because they are so adaptable in the kitchen, zucchini are probably the most popular Italian vegetable. My favourite way to eat zucchini fresh from the garden is to boil them for several minutes, slice them in half, dress with extra-virgin olive oil and lemon and sprinkle with chopped fresh tarragon. Every Italian region has its recipes for baked, sautéed, stuffed and fried zucchini. A classic is *zucchini al funghetto*, which means "zucchini cooked as if they were mushrooms". You slice them thinly and sauté for about five minutes in olive oil, garlic and parsley, with maybe a little anchovy and a dash of wine added. Amazingly, cooked in this way zucchini take on some of the consistency and flavour of mushrooms.

Every gardener who grows zucchini knows that their abundance can get out of hand. I meet this challenge by lightly deep-frying them and serve as a crisp appetizer. I also add them to salads, peeled and marinated in balsamic vinegar. Zucchini are also ideal for moulds and casseroles, combined with tomatoes.

A zucchini culinary plus are their large, yellowish-orange, edible flowers. I fry these in a light batter or stuff them with a little ricotta or piece of mozzarella cheese and some chopped herbs and sauté them in olive oil.

ZUCCHINI AND PASTA
Pasta e zucchine

6 TBSP EXTRA-VIRGIN OLIVE OIL
3 GARLIC CLOVES, CHOPPED
600G/1¼LB ZUCCHINI, TRIMMED AND
THINLY SLICED
600G/1¼LB PASTA, SUCH AS PENNE
1 HANDFUL FRESH BASIL LEAVES
6 TBSP GRATED PARMESAN CHEESE
SALT AND PEPPER

Heat the oil and garlic in a large pan, add the zucchini and sauté over a low heat, stirring often, for about 10 minutes, or until tender. Meanwhile, bring a large saucepan of water to the boil. Add the pasta and a little salt to the pan and cook until al dente. Drain the pasta, add to the zucchini, sprinkle with the basil and the Parmesan cheese and sauté for about 2 minutes over a medium heat. Check the salt, add pepper to taste and arrange on a platter. Serve immediately, very hot.

Serves 6

ZUCCHINI FILLED WITH HAM
Zucchine ripiene al prosciutto

1KG/2¼LB ZUCCHINI, TRIMMED
1 HANDFUL FRESH BREADCRUMBS
240ML/8FL OZ/1 CUP MILK
150G/5OZ HAM, FINELY CHOPPED
4 TBSP GRATED PARMESAN CHEESE
2 EGG YOLKS
2 TBSP FINELY CHOPPED FRESH
TARRAGON
2 TBSP EXTRA-VIRGIN OLIVE OIL
SALT AND PEPPER

Preheat the oven to 170°C/350°F/gas mark 3.

Halve each zucchini lengthwise and scoop out the flesh, to obtain oval cups. Soak the breadcrumbs in the milk for about 10 minutes then squeeze dry. Add the ham to the breadcrumbs with the Parmesan cheese and the egg yolks. Add salt and pepper to taste and the tarragon. Mix to blend well and fill the zucchini cavities with the mixture. Pour the oil into a baking dish and arrange the zucchini in the dish. Cook for about 1 hour, adding a little water from time to time. Arrange the zucchini on a platter and serve. They are also excellent cold.

Serves 6

ZUCCHINI CUTLETS

ZUCCHINE IN COSTOLETTA

1KG/2¼LB ZUCCHINI, TRIMMED
120G/4OZ/1 CUP PLAIN
(ALL-PURPOSE) FLOUR
2 EGGS
240G/8OZ/2 CUPS FINELY GRATED
DRIED BREADCRUMBS
1 TBSP DRIED MINT
120ML/4FL OZ/½ CUP EXTRA-VIRGIN
OLIVE OIL
120G/4OZ/8 TBSP UNSALTED BUTTER
SALT AND PEPPER

Slice the zucchini horizontally. Roll them in the flour to coat evenly. Beat the eggs in a deep dish with salt and pepper to taste. Put the breadcrumbs in another deep dish and add the mint. Dip the zucchini slices, a few at a time, in the egg mixture and roll them in the breadcrumbs until well coated. Heat the oil and butter in a large non-stick frying pan and fry the zucchini in a single layer, for about 3 minutes. Turn them gently and fry on the other side, until barely golden. Drain on kitchen paper and serve immediately, while very hot and crunchy.

Serves 6

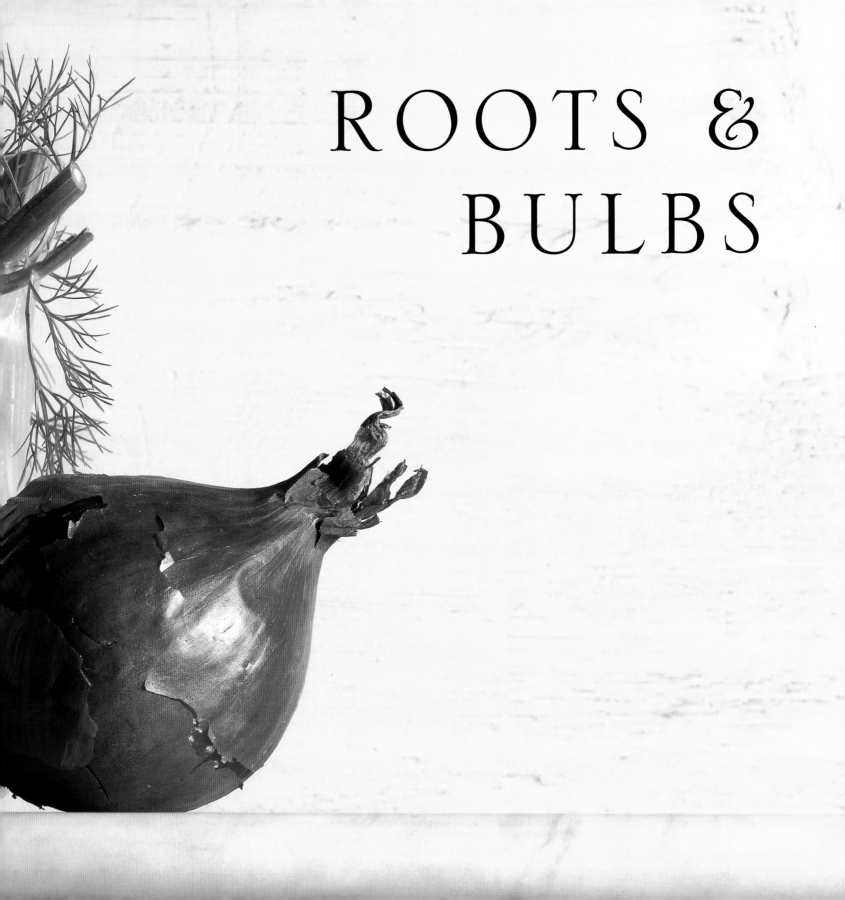

ROOTS & BULBS

CELERIAC

(APIUM GRAVEOLENS RAPACEUM)

Whenever I go to France I indulge once, but only once, in *celeri en remoulade* – blanched celery root served cold in a rich mayonnaise sauce seasoned with Dijon mustard. I have a friend from the Alsace region who adds gherkins, capers, garlic, herbs, a little anchovy and chopped hard-boiled (hard-cooked) egg – typically and deliciously French and definitely un-Italian. Although popular in most European countries, celeriac, or celery root, for some reason unknown to me, has never been popular in Italy, notwithstanding that celery stalk is a culinary staple. In books, I have come across only one recipe, from the Veneto region, that uses *sedano rapa*, celeriac, in a hearty soup combined with potatoes.

The fleshy root of the celery plant, about the size of a small turnip, sweeter and milder in flavour than the stalk, is now cultivated as a separate crop plant from bunch celery. It is good both raw and cooked. For salads I slice it raw and dress with lemon juice, extra-virgin olive oil and cracked black pepper. It combines well with cheese, especially Parmesan, which I shave paper-thin over the top. I also include freshly grated Parmesan in a white sauce for dressing boiled celeriac. It adds a savoury finish to the dish.

You will have to remove the top and bottom and tough skin on the sides of fresh celery root before cooking. As its flesh discolours very quickly, you must place the root in acidulated water as soon as it is peeled.

CELERIAC AND CHEESE SALAD
INSALATA DI SEDANO RAPA E PARMIGIANO REGGIANO

480G/1LB CELERIAC, TRIMMED AND
PEELED
1 TBSP LEMON JUICE
6 TBSP EXTRA-VIRGIN OLIVE OIL
210G/7OZ PIECE PARMESAN CHEESE
SALT AND PEPPER

Cut the celeriac into julienne strips and arrange in a salad bowl. Pour on the lemon juice, salt and pepper to taste and the oil and toss gently. Slice the Parmesan cheese paper thin, sprinkle on top of the salad and serve. A good-quality Emmenthal or Gruyère can be substituted for the Parmesan.

Serves 6

124

CELERIAC WITH A CREAMY SAUCE
SEDANO RAPA ALLA CREMA

1KG/2¼LB CELERIAC, TRIMMED
AND PEELED
25G/1OZ/2 TBSP UNSALTED BUTTER
2 TBSP PLAIN (ALL-PURPOSE) FLOUR
480ML/16FL OZ/2 CUPS MILK
3 TBSP WHITE VERMOUTH
6 TBSP FRESHLY GRATED
PARMESAN CHEESE
SALT AND PEPPER

Preheat the oven to 180°C/375°F/gas mark 4.

Cut the celeriac into thin slices and cook in boiling, salted water for about 15 minutes until tender, then drain. Heat 1 tablespoon of the butter in a saucepan, add the flour and cook over a medium heat, stirring with a wooden spoon, for about 3 minutes. Add the milk a little at a time, stirring continuously, until a creamy, white sauce is formed. Remove from the heat, add the remaining butter, the vermouth, Parmesan cheese and salt and pepper to taste. Mix until well blended. Arrange the celeriac on an ovenproof dish, cover with the sauce and cook in the oven for about 20 minutes, or until barely golden. Serve immediately.

Serves 6

CELERIAC WITH EGG AND LEMON SAUCE
SEDANO RAPA IN FRICASSEA

3 CELERIACS, TRIMMED AND PEELED
120ML/4FL OZ/½ CUP DRY WHITE WINE
3 TBSP EXTRA-VIRGIN OLIVE OIL
2 LARGE EGG YOLKS
2 TBSP LEMON JUICE
1 TBSP FINELY CHOPPED CHIVES
SALT

Cut the celeriac into julienne strips and arrange in a large saucepan. Reserve 3 tablespoons of the wine. Pour the remaining wine and the oil over the celeriac. Add salt to taste, cover and cook over a low heat for about 20 minutes until soft. Remove from the heat. Beat the egg yolks with the remaining wine and the lemon juice, add the chives and pour on to the celeriac. Toss gently, arrange on a platter and serve.

Serves 6

FENNEL

(FOENICULUM VULGARE)

FENNEL MIGHT NOT BE the most Italian of all vegetables but it is in Italy that the culinary qualities of this plant are most appreciated. In France it is known as Florence Fennel. It seems probable that Caterina de'Medici brought it with her when she left Florence for France on her way to marry the future King Henry II. In Italian it is called *finocchio*, which means "fine eye". According to Renaissance medical theory, eating it improved one's vision. Botanically it belongs to the carrot family, another vegetable reputed to be good for the eyes.

On Italian soil and on the Italian table the fennel plant appears in several forms. Wild fennel, *finocchiella* or *finocchietto*, produces stalks that grow up to 2 metres/6 feet high and bloom in tiny yellow flowers. These are picked, tied into little bouquets and hung in the pantry. The dried flowers are crumbled over dishes, especially to flavour pork. Left on the plant, the flowers go to seed and are used as seasoning in cooking and conserving. A regional Tuscan salami called *finocchiona* is studded with fennel seeds. The plant has feathery fronds that are added to salads and soups and *mariandes*, especially for fish. This fern-like foliage also makes an attractive garnish. Cultivated fennel is similar to the wild variety, except that the leaves swell to form pale green to white bulbs.

Fresh fennel is wonderfully aromatic, with a sweet and delicate anise flavour. The juicy bulb is excellent eaten raw on its own, thinly sliced and dressed simply with extra-virgin olive oil and lemon, or in combination with other raw vegetables and greens. It can be cooked in dozens of different ways, boiled, braised and baked. It enhances the flavour of almost any food. That is why my recipe for fennel sauce is so useful. In southern Italy fennel is usually combined with pasta and fish dishes. Tuscan cooks use it to flavour *arista*, roast loin of pork. In the north, cooks combine it, boiled or baked, with their regional cheese, Parmesan in particular.

While fresh, firm fennel bulbs are aromatic and juicy, nothing is so disappointing as bulbs that have dried out. In Italy, cultivated fennel begins to come on the market in late spring to early summer. This early season fennel is the best type to eat raw.

RICE AND FENNEL CAKE
TORTA DI RISO AL FINOCCHIO

600ML/1 PINT/2 CUPS MILK
180G/6OZ/1 CUP ARBORIO RICE
2 FENNEL BULBS, TRIMMED AND CHOPPED
120G/4OZ/½ CUP CASTER (SUPERFINE) SUGAR
3 EGGS
15G/½OZ/1 TBSP UNSALTED BUTTER
4 TBSP FINE DRIED BREADCRUMBS

Preheat the oven to 170°C/350°F/gas mark 3.

In a large saucepan, bring the milk to the boil, add the rice and fennel and cook over a low heat for about 30 minutes, stirring occasionally. Cool slightly then add the sugar and mix well. Add the eggs, one at a time. Butter a 23cm/9in springform tin and sprinkle with the breadcrumbs. Fill with the fennel mixture and cook for about 50 minutes. Cool for about 20 minutes, then unmould on to a platter and serve lukewarm or at room temperature.

Serves 6

FENNEL SAUCE
SALSA DI FINOCCHIO

3 FENNEL BULBS, TRIMMED
2 TBSP EXTRA-VIRGIN OLIVE OIL
120ML/4FL OZ/½ CUP MILK
1 TBSP FENNEL SEEDS
SALT AND PEPPER

Slice the fennel roughly and wash well. Place in a saucepan with the oil and milk, add salt and pepper to taste, cover and bring to a slow boil. Cook for about 10 minutes until tender, then purée in a blender. Reheat, adding a little water if necessary to thin to a creamy consistency. Sprinkle with the fennel seeds and serve with a pork roast, or with pasta.

Makes about 600ml/1 pint/2 cups of sauce

FENNEL WITH CHIVES
FINOCCHI ALL'ERBA CIPOLLINA

6 FENNEL BULBS, TRIMMED AND QUARTERED
4 TBSP EXTRA-VIRGIN OLIVE OIL
120ML/4FL OZ/½ CUP VERY LIGHT CHICKEN STOCK
3 TBSP CHIVES, FINELY CHOPPED
1 TBSP GRATED ORANGE ZEST
SALT AND PEPPER

Wash the fennel and place in a large saucepan with the oil and chicken stock. Add salt and pepper to taste, cover and cook over a low heat for about 20 minutes. Uncover and cook gently until any remaining liquid has evaporated. Arrange on a platter, sprinkle with the chives and orange zest and serve immediately.

Serves 6

GARLIC

(ALLIUM SATIVUM)

So EMPHATIC AM I during my cooking classes that garlic be used in moderation, many students get the impression I have something against it. On the contrary. I am a devotee of the "stinking rose" as the Elizabethan English referred to this most strongly scented and powerfully flavoured member of the onion family. Garlic is an important, even an essential ingredient in Italian cooking but it should always (or almost always) subtly flavour rather than overwhelm a dish. I shall mention several exceptions from the rule below. Perhaps I am reacting to a misconception I still come across when I travel abroad, namely that all you need do to make a dish "Italian" is add loads of garlic.

In Italy we plant garlic in early winter and it is ready to be harvested and dried by late spring. Dried garlic is used in the kitchen all year round but in the spring we have the passing pleasure of tasting fresh, green, still immature, garlic. I pull mine from the garden around Easter time. It also shows up in local markets but it is not commercially harvested in large quantities. Green garlic looks a little like a leek or spring onion (scallion), a green stalk with barely a suggestion of a fleshy, tender bulb at the root end. It is highly aromatic and

mildly flavoured. I use it especially in soups, salads and purées and to flavour roast meats.

Travelling around the world, I have had the opportunity to taste many varieties of garlic, whose skin colours range from white to rose to deep purple. The intensity of flavour also graduates from mild to hot. In California I came across a type called "Italian red" but here in Italy you normally find only white and rose-tinted varieties, medium strength in taste. Mature garlic is tastiest in the several months after its harvest. From June through the autumn it has a sweet, rich flavour. In the winter it develops a slightly bitter, harsh taste, but is still good, with care and moderation, for cooking.

For those of us who enjoy the pure taste of garlic, one of the best ways to appreciate its aroma and flavour is rubbed onto a piece of warm, grilled bread drizzled with extra-virgin olive oil. Many pasta sauces are centred on garlic. One in particular, called aglio, olio e peperoncino, "garlic, olive oil and chilli", allows you to indulge in as much garlic as you like. Many cooks include a generous amount of garlic in their recipe for pesto, along with this sauce's other ingredients, basil, olive oil, Parmesan and pine nuts.

GARLIC AND CHEESE TOASTS
Crostoni all'aglio

150G/5OZ FONTINA CHEESE, SLICED
240ML/8FL OZ/1 CUP MILK
6 SLICES COARSE-TEXTURED COUNTRY BREAD
6 GARLIC CLOVES
6 SLICES PLUM TOMATO

Put the cheese into a bowl, cover with the milk and place in the refrigerator overnight. When ready to serve, preheat the grill. Brush the bread on both sides with the garlic, drain the cheese and arrange on the bread. Cover with the tomato slices and cook under the grill for about 5 minutes, or until barely golden on top. Arrange the bread on a platter and serve immediately.

Serves 6

GARLIC SAUCE
CREMA DI AGLIO

6 GARLIC HEADS

120ML/4FL OZ/½ CUP EXTRA-VIRGIN OLIVE OIL

2 SMALL FRESH ZUCCHINI

1 TBSP FINELY CHOPPED FLAT-LEAF ITALIAN PARSLEY

SALT AND PEPPER

Preheat the oven to 180°C/375°F/gas mark 4.

Arrange the garlic heads on a baking dish, sprinkle with a little of the oil, add 240ml/8fl oz/1 cup water and cook for about 40 minutes. Using your fingers, squeeze the pulp from the cloves into a blender. Add the remaining oil, the zucchini, parsley and salt and pepper to taste and purée until creamy. Serve with pasta or on boiled vegetables.

Serves 6

GARLIC AND ROSEMARY PASTA
PASTA ALL'AGLIO E ROSMARINO

600G/1¼LB SHORT PASTA, SUCH AS PENNE OR RIGATONI

120ML/4FL OZ/½ CUP EXTRA-VIRGIN OLIVE OIL

12 GARLIC CLOVES

3 ROSEMARY SPRIGS

SALT AND PEPPER

Bring a large saucepan of water to the boil, add salt and the pasta and cook until just al dente. While the pasta is cooking, heat the oil in a pan. Finely chop the garlic and rosemary, add salt and pepper to taste and fry over a medium heat for about 3 minutes, or until the garlic is barely golden. Drain the pasta, keeping 3 tablespoons of the cooking water, and add both to the frying pan. Sauté, stirring continuously, for a couple of minutes, then arrange the pasta on a platter and serve very hot.

Serves 6

LEEKS

(ALLIUM PORRUM)

"By this leek, I will most horribly revenge. I eat and eat, I swear."

(WILLIAM SHAKESPEARE 1564–1616, HENRY VI PT II)

LEEKS, *ALLIUM PORRUM* in Latin and *porri* in Italian, like garlic, another member of the onion family, are cultivated for their stem rather than for their root. The ancient Romans highly esteemed the leek. They thought it worthy to serve on its own, whereas they used onions only for seasoning. In the only cookery book to survive from classical times, which is usually referred to by the name of the Roman gastronome Apicius, there are several recipes for cooking leeks. Tradition has it the Emperor Nero was so fond of them that he downed several bowls of leek soup daily in the belief that it improved his vocal if not his fiddling talents. The favourite dish of the poet Horace was pasta with leeks and chick peas. The Renaissance chef and recipe writer Bartolomeo Scappi prepared a contemporary-sounding leek and onion soup for his employer, a rich Roman cardinal.

Farmers bank up the soil to keep the stalk of the leek white and straight and cylindrical in shape. Left to themselves leeks can grow to considerable size, and in areas of Europe where they are cultivated, competitions are held for the largest leek.

Leeks that come to market are usually about 25.5cm/10in long and 5cm/2in thick. In late summer and early autumn I enjoy eating smaller leeks from my garden. I brush them with extra-virgin olive oil and cook them over a grill or steam them and dress with olive oil and plenty of cracked black pepper. At this early stage they are also tasty raw, cut into little rounds and seasoned with a vinaigrette or added to a mixed salad.

Leeks have a particularly pleasing flavour, not unlike an onion but sweeter and milder, and their taste blends beautifully with other ingredients. This quality makes them ideal for savoury tarts and soups. My favourite fish restaurant sometimes serves the catch of the day on a bed of braised leeks. Most Italian recipes for leeks come from the northern regions. I once heard them referred to as "the poor man's asparagus", and they are often cooked in many of the same ways, with melted butter and cheese. My recipe for leeks with fried eggs is a quick and easy way to make a tasty family supper.

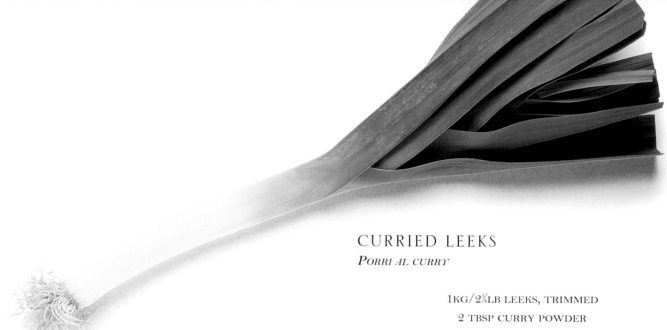

CURRIED LEEKS
PORRI AL CURRY

1KG/2¼LB LEEKS, TRIMMED

2 TBSP CURRY POWDER

1 BAY LEAF

4 TBSP EXTRA-VIRGIN OLIVE OIL

1 HANDFUL SULTANAS, SOFTENED IN WATER AND DRIED

1 APPLE, PEELED AND SLICED PAPER THIN

120ML/4FL OZ/½ CUP DRY WHITE WINE

SALT

Cut a slit down through the green leaves of the leeks, open them slightly and wash them well. Arrange in one layer in a large saucepan. Sprinkle with the curry powder, add the bay leaf, oil, sultanas and the apple slices. Add salt to taste, pour over the wine, cover and bring to a slow boil. Cook for about 20 minutes, or until tender, then uncover the pan and cook until any remaining liquid has evaporated. Arrange on a platter and serve.

Serves 6

LEEKS WITH FRIED EGGS
PORRI CON LE UOVA AL PADELLINO

1KG/2¼LB LEEKS, TRIMMED

90G/3OZ/6 TBSP UNSALTED BUTTER

6 LARGE EGGS

6 TBSP FRESHLY GRATED FONTINA CHEESE

1 TSP SWEET PAPRIKA

SALT

Cut a slit down through the green leaves of the leeks, open them slightly and wash them well. Bring a large saucepan of salted water to the boil, immerse the leeks and cook for about 10 minutes, or until tender. Drain and arrange on a platter and keep them hot. Melt the butter in a large pan, add the eggs and cook sunny-side up until the white is set. Sprinkle a little salt on to the egg whites and arrange the eggs on the white part of the leeks. Sprinkle with the grated Parmesan cheese, pour over the butter from the pan, sprinkle with the paprika and serve.

Serves 6

LEEKS WITH PARMESAN CHEESE
PORRI ALLA PARMIGIANA

1KG/2¼LB LEEKS, TRIMMED
90G/3OZ/6 TBSP UNSALTED BUTTER
6 TBSP GRATED PARMESAN CHEESE
SALT AND PEPPER

Cut a slit down through the green leaves of the leeks, open them slightly and wash them well. Bring a large saucepan of salted water to the boil, immerse the leeks and cook for about 10 minutes, or until tender. Drain and arrange on a platter and keep them warm. Meanwhile, melt the butter in a saucepan over a medium heat. Sprinkle the Parmesan over the leeks, pour on the butter and serve them immediately. You can also at this point place them under a very hot grill for a few minutes or until the Parmesan becomes golden.

Serves 6

ONIONS

(ALLIUM CEPA)

> *"Life is like an onion, which one peels crying."*
>
> (FRENCH PROVERB)

IT IS INCONCEIVABLE to think of cooking Italian dishes without the ubiquitous onion, *Allium cepa*, so basic and indispensable is it to practically every dish. From reading and travelling over the years, I have the impression this is true also for most other cuisines of the world. There is archeological evidence that onions, probably originally from Asia, have been cultivated and eaten since prehistoric times. In Italy the primary culinary function of the onion, *cipolla*, is to subtly add its flavour, roughly chopped and slowly sautéed in olive oil with celery and carrot, to the traditional *soffritto*, the first and fundamental step in most Italian recipes. It is also featured on its own as the main ingredient in many regional recipes.

Dozens of types of onion are commonly available, from tiny white ones to big, beautifully coloured purple varieties. I begin to pull up spring onions (scallions) from my garden usually around Easter time when their bulbs have barely begun to bulge. They are still green but sweet and delicately flavoured. I add them to spring greens salads. They are also tasty grilled, seasoned with olive oil and good balsamic vinegar.

By late spring and into midsummer we have smooth, tender-skinned white, yellow and purple onions with large bulbs. The fresh red onions are sweetest and I use them raw in salads. The yellow ones are best for cooking and I often stuff them with a savoury mixture of meat and cheese. This is also the season for *cipolline*, a type of small onion I have never seen outside of Italy, thin and rather flat in shape, which are ideal for sweet and sour preparations. I have included a recipe using red wine vinegar and chocolate – a combination of flavours redolent of the Renaissance.

By late autumn there are no more fresh onions at market, so I must begin to bring cured ones with dried skins from the larder, where they have been left after harvesting for winter use. When I was a child, I remember family outings in Piedmont, when my parents would buy onions roasted in braziers along country roads for a midday snack. Roasted onions with their skins intact and ready to eat are still sold in markets. All you need do is peel, slice and season them with very good extra-virgin olive oil and, for added flavour, a few drops of fine balsamic vinegar.

ONION CREAM WITH CORIANDER
CREMA DI CIPOLLE AL CORIANDOLO

3 TBSP EXTRA-VIRGIN OLIVE OIL
1KG/2¼LB ONIONS, PEELED AND SLICED
1 LITRE/1¾ PINT/4 CUPS VERY LIGHT CHICKEN STOCK
120G/4OZ/¾ CUP FRESHLY GRATED PARMESAN CHEESE
2 TBSP FRESH CORIANDER LEAVES, FINELY CHOPPED
SALT AND PEPPER

Heat the oil in a saucepan and cook the onions, covered, over a low heat for about 20 minutes, until translucent, stirring occasionally. Add the stock and continue to cook for 1 hour more. Purée in a foodmill or blender and reheat, adding a little water if necessary to thin the soup. Pour into a soup tureen, mix in the Parmesan, sprinkle with the coriander and serve immediately.

Serves 6

PEARL ONIONS WITH CHOCOLATE
CIPOLLINE AL CIOCCOLATO

3 TBSP EXTRA-VIRGIN OLIVE OIL
1KG/2¼LB BABY (PEARL) ONIONS, PEELED
2 TBSP CASTER (SUPERFINE) SUGAR
2 TBSP PLAIN (BITTERSWEET) CHOCOLATE, GRATED
60ML/2FL OZ/¼ CUP RED WINE VINEGAR
SALT AND PEPPER

Heat the oil in a pan and cook the onions over a low heat for about 20 minutes, or until golden, shaking the pan from time to time. Add the sugar, chocolate, vinegar and salt and pepper to taste, cover and cook for 10 minutes more, adding a little water if necessary to keep the bottom of the pan moist. Arrange the onions on a platter and serve.

Serves 6

ONION FILLED WITH HAM
CIPOLLE AL PROSCIUTTO

6 LARGE ONIONS, RED OR YELLOW,
UNPEELED
120G/4OZ HAM, FINELY CHOPPED
6 TBSP FRESHLY GRATED
PARMESAN CHEESE
1 LARGE EGG
1 HANDFUL FRESH BREADCRUMBS,
SOAKED IN MILK AND SQUEEZED DRY
25G/1OZ/2 TBSP UNSALTED BUTTER
4 TBSP VERY LIGHT CHICKEN STOCK
SALT AND PEPPER

Preheat the oven to 180°C/375°F/gas mark 4.

Bring a large saucepan of water to the boil, add the onions and cook for about 10 minutes. Drain, rinse under cold water then peel them. Halve each onion and scoop out the flesh to make a hollow. In a bowl, mix the ham with the Parmesan cheese, egg, breadcrumbs and salt and pepper to taste. Fill the onions with this mixture and top each with a dot of butter. Grease a baking dish with the remaining butter and arrange the onions in the dish. Pour in the stock and cook in the oven for about 50 minutes, or until tender and slightly golden on top. Arrange on a platter and serve.

Serves 6

CARROTS

(DAUCUS CAROTA SATIVA)

"The day is coming when a single carrot, freshly observed,
will set off a revolution."

(PAUL CÉZANNE 1836–1906)

LIKE BEETROOT, the carrot, another root, was originally purplish red. This is how it was first described in the twelfth century by an Arab naturalist writing from Andalusia in southern Spain.

Orange carrots begin to appear in Dutch still-life paintings of the seventeenth century. They had been cultivated in the Netherlands for several generations. The colour comes from a pigment that is the source of vitamin A and their much celebrated salubrious effects.

Because of their high sugar content, in the medieval and Renaissance periods carrots were prized as a sweetener for desserts. Carrot cake, which seemed a novelty when it became popular in the 1960s, was really a revival of an ancient recipe. In Italy carrots have been most commonly used as an aromatic ingredient, along with celery and onion, for the traditional *soffritto*, which forms a base to enrich sauces, marinades and stocks for soups. Today they are also appreciated on their own or combined with another congenial vegetable, like turnips.

I look forward in late spring to the first tiny carrots harvested from my garden. Much of a carrot's flavour is in its skin and at this stage they do not have to be peeled. They are wonderfully fresh and crisp eaten raw as part of a vegetable *antipasto* (I sometimes serve them with a savory yogurt and horseradish dip) or cooked al dente and dressed with a little butter. Further on in their season carrots become sweeter and then they are good grated or sliced and served in a salad. I like to combine them with the first table grapes, dressed with lemon juice and extra-virgin olive oil. At the end of their season, when they have developed a hard core, I slice them thinly and make a carrot fricassee, served with an egg and lemon sauce.

CARROTS AND GRAPE SALAD
INSALATA DI CAROTE E UVA

480G/1LB CARROTS, TRIMMED
300G/10OZ BLACK GRAPES, WASHED
AND DRIED
6 TBSP EXTRA-VIRGIN OLIVE OIL
1 TBSP LEMON JUICE
SALT AND PEPPER

Peel and wash the carrots then cut them into julienne strips and place in a salad bowl. Add the grapes, oil, lemon juice and salt and pepper to taste. Mix gently and serve.
Serves 6

CARROTS WITH LEMON SAUCE
CAROTE IN FRICASSEA

1KG/2¼LB CARROTS, TRIMMED
3 TBSP EXTRA-VIRGIN OLIVE OIL
2 EGG YOLKS
JUICE OF 1 LEMON
2 TBSP FINELY CHOPPED FLAT-LEAF ITALIAN PARSLEY
SALT AND PEPPER

Peel and wash the carrots and slice them thinly crosswise. Heat the oil in a saucepan, add the carrots and mix well. Add a little water, lower the heat to minimum, cover and cook, stirring occasionally, for about 20 minutes, or until tender. Beat the egg yolks with the lemon juice and a little water. Remove the pan from the heat, add salt and pepper to taste, then the parsley and the egg mixture. Stir to blend the flavours then arrange on a platter and serve.

Serves 6

CARROTS WITH YOGURT DIP

CAROTE IN SALSA PICCANTE

12 BABY CARROTS, PEELED, TRIMMED
AND WASHED
120ML/4FL OZ/½ CUP YOGURT
3 TBSP EXTRA-VIRGIN OLIVE OIL
1 TBSP FINELY CHOPPED FLAT-LEAF
ITALIAN PARSLEY
2 TBSP FINELY GRATED
FRESH HORSERADISH
SALT

Place the carrots in a bowl of water and ice in the refrigerator for about 2 hours – this will make them crunchier. Drain and slice in half vertically. Mix the yogurt, oil, parsley, horseradish and salt to taste in a bowl. Arrange the carrots around the sides of the bowl and serve them to be dipped in the sauce.

Serves 6

145

PARSNIPS & TURNIPS

(PASTINACA SATIVA)

"*There is a Southern proverb – fine words butter no parsnips.*"

(SIR WALTER SCOTT 1771–1832, *THE LEGEND OF MONTROSE*, CH. 3)

IF YOU ASK AN ITALIAN what a *pastinaca* or parsnip is, almost certainly he or she would not know and might guess it to be a new kind of pasta machine. In northern regions where parsnips were cultivated as fodder for animals, farmers referred to them as *carote bianche*, white carrots. They were popular in the medieval period, as a source of starch before the potato was brought to Europe from America and as a culinary sweetener in times when sugar was rare and costly. Now in Italy the potato and the carrot have superseded the parsnip. I have eaten parsnips in England and rather liked their somewhat odd but distinctive semi-sweet, nutty flavour. The recipe for parsnip purée is good alongside roast game and meats.

You are not likely to see turnips in most Italian markets either, maybe a few in the north. *Minestra di riso e rape*, rice and turnip soup, is a traditional dish from the region of Lombardy, of which Milan is the capital, the city where I was born. So unlike most of the rest of Italians, who probably have never tasted a turnip, I learned to like them when I was young. In Friuli-Venezia Giulia, in the north-eastern corner of Italy on the border with Austria and Yugoslavia, they make a regional relish with turnips called *brovade*. The turnips are marinated for a month under wine pressings, the dregs left over from wine making. *Brovade* is typically served with local salami.

The radish, *rapanello*, a relation of the turnip, is much more popular in Italian vegetable gardens and markets. It is often served as an antipasto, to munch on its own, or as part of a salad. Nothing is quite so satisfying as biting into a small, young, spring radish, perfectly crisp and slightly peppery hot. The radishes we grow in Italy are brilliant red with bright green tops. They are either perfectly round or oval shaped. In other parts of the world radishes come in assorted colours, shapes and sizes. Still, I have tasted nothing that surpasses the burst of flavour I get from a small, simple radish, fresh from my garden.

RADISHES AND GREEN RADICCHIO SALAD

INSALATA DI RAPANELLI E RADICCHIO

210G/7OZ ROUND RED RADISHES,
WASHED AND SLICED PAPER THIN
300G/10OZ GREEN RADICCHIO,
WASHED AND CUT INTO SHREDS
1 TBSP RED WINE VINEGAR
4 TBSP EXTRA-VIRGIN OLIVE OIL
SALT

Place the radishes and radicchio in a salad bowl and mix well. Dissolve the salt with the vinegar, add the oil and pour on to the salad. Toss together gently and serve.

Serves 6

PARSNIP PUREE
PUREA DI PASTINACHE

480G/1LB PARSNIPS, TRIMMED AND PEELED
480G/1LB POTATOES
40G/1½OZ/3 TBSP UNSALTED BUTTER
240ML/8FL OZ/1 CUP MILK
2 TBSP CHIVES, CHOPPED
SALT AND PEPPER

Dice the parsnips and cook in boiling, salted water until tender. Cover the potatoes with water, add salt and bring to the boil. Cook until tender then drain and peel. Pass them, while still warm, through a ricer with the parsnips. Pour the purée into a saucepan and mix until well blended. Add the butter, milk and salt and pepper to taste and reheat, stirring constantly. Pour the purée on to a platter, sprinkle with the chives and serve.

Serves 6

RICE AND TURNIP SOUP
MINESTRA DI RISO E RAPE

480G/1LB TURNIPS, TRIMMED AND PEELED
60G/2OZ/4 TBSP UNSALTED BUTTER
12 HANDFULS ARBORIO RICE
2 LITRE/3½ PINT/8 CUPS LIGHT CHICKEN STOCK
6 TBSP FRESHLY GRATED PARMESAN CHEESE
SALT AND PEPPER

Wash and slice the turnips then dice them into tiny cubes. Melt the butter in a large saucepan, add the rice and cook, stirring continuously, for about 3 minutes. Meanwhile, heat the chicken stock to boiling point. Add the turnips to the rice, stir to blend the flavours, then add the boiling stock and simmer for 15 minutes. Add salt and pepper to taste, and pour into a soup tureen. Serve with the Parmesan cheese sprinkled on top.

Serves 6

POTATOES

(SOLANUM TUBEROSUM)

> "I've a head like a concertina, I've a tongue like a button-stick,
> I've a mouth like an old potato, and I'm more than a little sick."

(RUDYARD KIPLING 1865–1936, *CELLS*)

THE HUMBLE POTATO, second, perhaps, only to the tomato, is one of the great gastronomic blessings brought to the European table from the Americas by sixteenth-century explorers. It would seem from reading old recipe books that it took a while for the potato to become popular in Italy. Only in the late nineteenth century did it take on the status of a staple. The northern regions favored rice and southerners preferred their pasta. Now potatoes are cooked with care and eaten with enthusiasm up and down the peninsula. I have friends from other countries who tell me their children rate the "French Fries" of Italy, *patatine*, the best in the world. A good part of the credit must go to our extra-virgin olive oil and the frying skills of our cooks.

Although grown beneath the ground, potatoes are not really roots but rather vine tubers formed underground. The varieties cultivated over the centuries on all five continents are numerous. In Italy we favour the so-called waxy types, whose texture holds up better in most preparations, over the floury kinds preferred in England and America. I most look forward in early summer to "new potatoes", early harvested immature potatoes with skin so delicate you don't need to peel them. I boil and dress new potatoes simply with extra-virgin olive oil and a sprinkle of parsley.

Italians cook potatoes in many ways, on their own and with other ingredients. Special mention must be given to the potato *gnocchi*, dumplings made with puréed potatoes, egg, and flour and dressed with butter and cheese. For years a favourite at my cooking classes has been a simple recipe for baking potatoes. All you do before baking is make a slice into the side of the potato, insert a bay leaf and coat with extra-virgin olive oil. When all is said and done, it is hard to top the tastiness of roast potatoes with rosemary done the way of Tuscan home cooks for centuries. Diced potatoes are first lightly and quickly fried in oil, seasoned with rosemary, garlic, salt and pepper. Then they are roasted in the oven for about an hour until they turn deep gold in colour. When you get it right, they will come out crispy on the outside and soft on the inside, aromatic and delicious.

POTATO GNOCCHI
Gnocchi di patate

1KG/2¼LB BAKING POTATOES, WASHED
BUT UNPEELED
210G/7OZ/⅔ CUPS PLAIN
(ALL-PURPOSE) FLOUR
1 EGG
PINCH OF GRATED NUTMEG
90G/3OZ/6 TBSP UNSALTED BUTTER
4 TBSP GRATED PARMESAN CHEESE
SALT AND PEPPER

Preheat the oven to 170°C/350°F/gas mark 3.

Wrap each damp potato in foil and cook them in the oven for about 1 hour, or until tender. Peel them immediately and pass them through a potato ricer into a bowl. Add half the flour, the egg, nutmeg and salt and pepper to taste, and mix well. With the remaining flour, dust the table and your hands. Roll the potato mixture into sausages about 1cm/½in thick and cut them into 2cm/⅜in lengths. With well-floured hands, form the sausages into walnut-shaped ovals and press them lightly with a fork in order to give them their traditional ridged pattern. Bring a large saucepan of salted water to the boil, immerse the gnocchi a few at a time and drain them with a slotted spoon as soon as they come to the surface. Arrange them on a hot platter. Meanwhile, melt the butter over a low heat in a saucepan and cook until golden brown. Sprinkle the cooked gnocchi with the Parmesan, pour the butter over them and serve immediately.

Serves 6

ROASTED POTATOES WITH ROSEMARY
Patate arrosto al rosmarino

1KG/2¼LB BAKING POTATOES, WASHED
AND PEELED
600ML/1 PINT/2 CUPS OIL FOR FRYING
3 ROSEMARY SPRIGS
6 GARLIC CLOVES
SALT AND PEPPER

Dice the potatoes into 2cm x 2cm/⅜in x ⅜in cubes. Place in a bowl, cover with water and leave for about 2 hours, then drain and pat dry.

Preheat the oven to 170°C/350°F/gas mark 3. Heat the oil in a non-stick roasting pan over a medium heat. Add the potatoes, rosemary, garlic and salt and pepper to taste and mix well. Cook until the potatoes are sizzling. Put the pan in the oven and cook for about 1 hour, turning them every 15 minutes, until dark golden and crispy on top. Drain them on paper towel, arrange on a platter and serve immediately.

Serves 6

POTATOES
WITH BAY LEAVES

PATATE ALL'ALLORO

18 SMALL POTATOES, WASHED
BUT UNPEELED
18 BAY LEAVES, FRESH OR DRIED
3 TBSP EXTRA-VIRGIN OLIVE OIL
SALT AND PEPPER

Preheat the oven to 170°C/350°F/gas mark 3.

Make a deep incision in the longest side of each potato, without cutting right through, and insert a bay leaf in the incision. Pour the oil into a baking dish and add a little salt and pepper to taste. Roll the potatoes in the oil until well coated, then cook them for about 50 minutes to 1 hour, until tender. Arrange the potatoes on a serving dish, leaving the bay leaf inside, and serve them hot. You can substitute the bay leaf with a rosemary sprig if you like.

Serves 6

BEETROOT

(BETA VULGARIS)

ITALY HAS ITS OWN VARIETY of beetroot, the Chioggia, named after its place of origin not far from the Venetian lagoon. It is a clear ruby red, its root swollen to the size of an orange and perfectly round in shape, with a relatively mild flavour. Other types of beetroot are coloured purple, pink, yellow and white. In size some are as large as a grapefruit and bitter in taste. Others have a cylindrical, elongated shape. They all have a high sugar content. Certain beet varieties are cultivated for their leafy, brilliant green tops, which have a mild flavour and are cooked like spinach and chard.

Red beet, which is sometimes known as Roman beet, is said to have been developed in the Mediterranean area, Italy, Greece and North Africa, in ancient times. However, it became most popular in the kitchens of northern and eastern Europe during the Middle Ages. Perhaps these people, living in cold and dark climates, were particularly attracted to its intense, scarlet colour, caused by the combination of a purple and yellow pigment in the root. At any rate the most famous of all beetroot dishes, borscht in its various forms, was developed in eastern Europe, the Ukraine in particular. This is a delicious sweet red (of course) soup, served hot or cold. The stock is made from meat and a dollop of sour cream is usually added on top before serving.

In Italy we most often use beetroot in salads. Their sweet, earthy flavour combines well with many other ingredients, in particular oranges, onions, fennel, endive and walnuts. The juxtaposition of slices of beets and blood oranges is strikingly colourful as well as tasty.

The best way to cook beetroot is to wrap them in foil and bake in the oven until tender. This method is very much preferable to boiling, which causes them to lose both colour and flavour. During their season, summer and autumn, beetroot arrive in Italian markets already roasted and still in their skins. When they are peeled and cut open, they start bleeding their highly coloured juice. For a quick and simple salad, I slice them and season with salt, vinegar and extra-virgin olive oil. If you buy raw beetroot when it is young and tender, you can boil the stems and leaves and serve them in a salad.

BEETROOT CREAM
PASSATO DI BARBABIETOLE

1KG/2¼LB BEETROOTS, TRIMMED

2 LITRE/3½ PINT/8 CUPS LIGHT

CHICKEN STOCK

210G/7OZ RICE

240ML/8FL OZ/1 CUP YOGURT

2 TBSP CHIVES, FINELY CHOPPED

SALT AND PEPPER

Peel and slice the beetroots and arrange them in a large saucepan with the stock and the rice and bring to the boil. Cook for about 1 hour over a low heat. Strain and cool slightly then purée in a blender. Add salt and pepper to taste. Reheat to boiling point then add half the yogurt and mix well. Pour into a soup tureen, dot with the remaining yogurt, sprinkle on the chives and serve.

Serves 6

BEETROOT SALAD
BARBABIETOLE IN INSALATA

1KG/ 2¼LB BEETROOTS, TRIMMED

2 ORANGES, PEELED AND SLICED

1 WHITE ONION, SLICED PAPER THIN

1 HARD-BOILED (HARD-COOKED) EGG, VERY FINELY CHOPPED

4 TBSP EXTRA-VIRGIN OLIVE OIL

SALT AND PEPPER

Preheat the oven to 180°C/375°F/gas mark 4.

Wash the beetroots well and wrap each one in a piece of foil. Cook them in the oven for about 1 hour. Let them cool then peel and slice them and arrange the slices on a platter. Add the orange slices to the beetroot and cover with the onion. Sprinkle the hard-boiled egg on top of the salad, then sprinkle with salt, pepper and olive oil and serve.

Serves 6

BEETROOTS WITH HORSERADISH SAUCE
BARBABIETOLE AL RAFANO

1KG/2¼LB BEETROOTS, TRIMMED

1 TBSP GRATED FRESH HORSERADISH

1 TBSP WORCESTERSHIRE SAUCE

60ML/2FL OZ/⅓ CUP FRESH DOUBLE

(HEAVY) CREAM

SALT

Preheat the oven to 180°C/375°F/gas mark 4.

Wash the beetroots well and wrap each one in a piece of foil. Cook them in the oven for about 1 hour. Let them cool then peel, dice and arrange in a salad bowl. Mix the horseradish with the Worcestershire sauce and cream and add salt to taste. Pour on to the beetroots, mix gently and serve.

Serves 6

INDEX

ACKNOWLEDGEMENTS

Mike Newton would like to thank the following individuals and organizations for their assistance in the photography for this book:

Jeanette and Graham at Tableprops, London, for props and backgrounds.
Additional styling, Helen Trent.

For help with supplying the vegetables:
Andy Georghiou at Macken and Collins, Chiswick, London,
Horti Halycon and Katheryn Dawson at Chiswick Farmers' Market,
Panzer, Swiss Cottage, London,
Vitacress Salads Limited, Andover.

Special thanks to Bridget Sargeson assisted by Vicki Keppel-Compton, for food preparation.

Vivien James and Nina Sharman at Pavilion Books.

David Fordham for his design.